The Way of an EAGLE

Charting Your Path to High Places in Christ

by
Vernon Percy Howard, Jr.

ISBN: 1-58597-256-8

Library of Congress Control Number: 2004091540

*To my loving wife, Frances, whose royalty
is unmistakable …*

*To my daughter, Sophia, whose
spark and creativity are uncontainable …*

*To my son, Vernon III, whose glee and
imagination are insurmountable.*

There are three things which are too wonderful for me,
Yes, four which I do not understand:
The way of an eagle in the air...

— *Proverbs 30:18-19*

Table of Contents

Acknowledgments

In Memoriam to Mac Charles Jones and Rowena Neely, eagles who taught me what it means to fly in contrary winds.

Thank you, Mamma Sherrell, for pushing me out, loving me and believing in me.

Thanks to Warren H. Stewart, Sr.; Thomas L. Clifton; Carolyn Gordon; Robert L. Stephens, Sr.; Steve Bland, Jr.; and Warren Anderson, Jr., for their care, nurture and expertise.

Thanks to Denise and Marion Jordon for their inspiration and encouragement.

Thanks also to Eric Belt, Desiree Davis, Michelle Hatcher and Thomas McAdams for their time and feedback.

Thanks to Pastor Daryl Henry for persistently asking me, "When...?"

Thanks to Ernest Tinsley and the brothers of the Men's Ministry of First Institutional Baptist Church in Phoenix, Arizona, for allowing me to flush some of this material out in prayer, reflection, preaching, teaching and workshop over the last three years. Keep on turning it around, brothers!

Thanks to Lizetta "Smitty" Smith, Tameka McLaughlin and the Mountaintop Family for their faithfulness during my times away.

Thanks to the Cook, Stepter, Chama, Tharpe, Cosby, Morton, Cobbler, Rodriguez, Jones, Baskin, McDow and Copeland families for cold water to drink in a dry place.

Thanks to my family at home — Frances, Brandi, Brandon, Sophia and Vernon III; Lonnie and Teresa Taylor; Chonita Taylor; Norma and Frank Neely; Thelma Glenn; Ned Stovall; LaMonica Howard; Mary McAdams, and a host of their seed for not leaving me without honor in my own home.

CHAPTER I

The Burden to Soar

HAUNTED BY THE HOLY GHOST

Deep within your spirit you know, and have known for some time, that there is a level and state of spiritual power and communion with God that you have yet to achieve. In the depths of your soul there is a hunger and longing to experience God in a new and fresh way. There may be much about your walk with God which has puzzled you to this point but there is one thing that you do know for sure — your current station and status will no longer do. You are burdened, shall I dare say "haunted" even by the Holy Ghost, to ascend to that level of communion and purpose in God which still escapes your walk. Face it! Deal with it! You are not satisfied with what you are doing for God, and the Holy Ghost continues to remind you that God is not getting full glory from your life, service or ministry. This is a burden that you can choose to try and ignore if you like, but it will be a weight that you will carry for the rest of your life because you know that God's plans and purposes for you are not being fulfilled in this season. Have you considered that maybe it's time for you to cease just walking with God and begin to soar with Him?

I am convinced that there are places where God visits, and this is good. But there are also places where God dwells continually, and this is better. There are places where God is present, and this is good. But then there are places where God is not only present but moving in His power and might, and this is awesome. There are places where God is sought after and this is noble; yet there are places which He is found in fullness, and this is glorious. Your burden is that you want the dwelling, not just the visitation. Your burden is that you want more than His presence, you want His awesome move. Your burden is that you want to live a life and practice ministry in the Kingdom in such a way that you go in and come out having said, "I have searched and He is found and it is glorious!" Stop thinking something is wrong with you or wrong with God. The only problem is you are haunted by the Holy Spirit who has convicted you to the point that you don't want to walk anymore! You want to soar!

I was awakened to the knowledge of this burden in my life a while back as God was transitioning me from things acquainted with to things unknown. The journey God sent me on separated me from the institutional structures and individual relationships that had contributed greatly in my formation as a minister. God separated me from the people, places and institutions that I had relied on for identity and purpose. Herein I learned that people and places can't give you true identity and purpose. They can only serve as the contexts where you live out and honor your identity and purpose. It was only in the departure from my hometown, the death of my mentor, the leaving of the first church I'd ever pastored and the temporary removal of myself from high positions in denominational bureaucracy that I found who *I* really was to become. And who I really was to become could only manifest itself as I discovered ***Him*** more fully.

No longer preaching to a thousand each Sunday and no longer paid a thousand-plus each Sunday, the Word of the Lord apprehended me as I was to deliver what turned out for me to be a life-changing message to the fifty warriors who carried out the vision for the new ministry God had led me to birth. I was in God's will and doing God's work, yet searching for that "more" that I knew deep in my spirit still escaped me. I came across these words of the Apostle Paul:

> *"And I know that when I come to you,*
> *I will come in the fullness of the blessing*
> *of the Gospel of Christ."*
> *— Romans 15:29*

God used this bold statement by Paul to apprehend me in a way that has unfolded only a handful of times in my life. As the deep meaning of this statement began to drench my spirit over time, it was as if I had heard something, was experiencing something or was going somewhere no one else had ever gone. And perhaps I was. I know for sure that God wanted to take me to a new level in Him. And often that's the way it is when God is producing a landmark moment in your journey. It's like something is going on that nobody else has privilege to see or encounter. I thought of Isaiah in the year that King Uzziah died as the prophet saw and experienced such a quaking vision that it set him on a life course and mission where God spoke through him the greatest prophetic oracles of the restoration of Israel at that time. Yet there is no record that anyone else in the temple heard or saw anything out of the ordinary. With all that Isaiah is recorded to have experienced on that day in worship, you would think that somebody else somewhere in the temple felt something shake. But there is no mention of it amid the mention of every other fine detail of his experience. This says to us you can never let the mundane of your environment hinder your belief in the work of the marvelous, especially when the marvelous is occurring in you. God endows certain people with the marvelous amid the mundane conditions where we operate so that once we've honored God's move nothing remains the same. This experience, Isaiah-like in a sense, was one of the rare occasions where God's visitation was so near, real and **awesome** and it took me to a new level of strength and illumination where God was unyielding as He ultimately spoke:

> **"Oh yes, I am an awesome God and what you are
> experiencing in Me is awesome …
> Now, I want you to learn how to *live under the awe!*"**

Living under the awe meant no more fading in and out of His purpose. Living under the awe meant no more temporary loss of God's vision for my life. Living under the awe meant no more doubting that I was who God said that I was. It meant no more looking cool and courageous by day, yet fearing for my well-being by night. It meant no more chronic shifting of my personality based on who was around, worrying about what they'd think or how they might not support my ministry if they didn't get a certain face. (Is there a witness?) Living under the awe meant no more fleeting, short-term meandering from the perfect and narrow road God had so ordered for each moment of my life. Living under the awe meant living in a way behind closed doors that was in perfect harmony with my actions during the day. It meant being pressed up against God like never before like a baby boy clinging to his father, not for life, but instead for *the* life. Not out of desperation, but in adoration, inspiration and restoration. Living under the awe meant no longer depending on my natural talents of charisma and persuasive charm. It meant instead trusting God's Spirit to work through the spiritual gifts He gave. It meant knowing that because I had been with Jesus already, standing to minister was only a continuation of my fellowship and worship so that I could say with confidence like Paul for any given ministry opportunity:

"I'm coming in the fullness."

I became burdened for this *"fullness"* Paul talked about. And I became burdened to experience the confident assurance he seemed to have had that wherever he went to stir his gifts and edify the church, there that fullness would be also. Yeah, I wanted that. I wanted to be real and true to the fullness that God wanted for me. Here it was ten years and many tears after I first began in ministry and I remember thinking to myself, "If I'm going to do this thing (ministry in the Kingdom of God), I want to do it right. I don't want to walk any more. I want to soar!

DEAL WITH IT!

But also, I had to decide what to do about what I wanted. Would I carry the burden or would I pretend that nothing ever happened? This is where many of us are in the Kingdom. We pretend we're not haunted. We pretend we haven't heard from God reminding us that there is something more. For you see, this burden is really only carried by those who possess the spiritual tenacity to say yes and continue to say yes daily, to the call of God upon our lives to carry out specific mission for the Kingdom. Everybody possesses the burden. Everybody is called to *fullness.* Everybody's preordained destiny is to soar. But not everybody is willing to carry the burden that strengthens us to fly.

Carrying the burden means living with the pressure of the call to spiritual excellence and divine purpose. This involves a continual standing before God and being measured out, broken down, changed, re-arranged and raised up to perform. Not as one who entertains, but as one who is more and more ready and effective to show forth the ever-increasing glory of God on earth.

Regrettably, many of us allow the overwhelming presence of criticism or the discomforting apathy of those near or far to set us back from dealing with our burden to soar. But neither the critic nor the apathetic carry sufficient weight of influence for us who are mounting up. The Apostle Paul clearly teaches us this. He was an anomaly in and of himself, kind of an odd and obscure fellow at the start who couldn't be trusted. He called himself an apostle, yet he didn't have the credentials of having walked with Jesus as the others. His legacy was the murder and stoning of those who followed the way of Christ, and yet overnight he literally turned to be one of those he led mobs in murdering. His indigenous religious community turned on him because he left their traditions. His newfound community saw him as shady and dangerous because he once tried to have them all killed. And the larger community just thought he was part of that little sect of Jews who went astray after some carpenter's son from Nazareth born out of wedlock in a barn over in Bethlehem who claimed to be the new king but had no weapons, chariots or armies and died without a battle for all to see. The criticism and apathy was pervasive. Yet he wrote two-thirds of the New Testament and planted and nurtured churches all over the then know Christendom. How? Why? Partly because he understood that his burden was his. He understood that the critics, though noisy with clammer, could not carry his burden born in the dust of the Damascus road. He knew that the apathetic, though silent and distant, were not acquainted with his burden nurtured and matured in the isolation of the Arabian desert.

Only you carry your load. Even when prayed for, encouraged or journeyed with, still there is a place where the burden hits you and none else. Over time you learn to tell the critics that they can rant and rave all they want. You learn to dismiss the apathetic all together from having influence on your journey. How many people miss the opportunities to rise up because they are focused on people who don't even care about them?

You are the one who's doing the fasting, praying and warring. You are the one who is stirring the gifts God gave. You are the one who is living a life sold out and sacrificed for King Jesus. You are the one who takes the risks. You are the one who gives the sweat. You are the one who had the courage to stand before God and depart from mediocrity, discard the ordinary and refrain from the regular. You are the one who made the decision to walk with God, now make the decision to soar with Him. And what does it matter if critics don't like the wave of your wings or the timing of your skyward mount?

What does it matter if those you thought loved you don't care enough to behold your soar? It is they who will miss the beauty of your flight. But as for you, you have mountaintops to peak.

We must deal with it! And we must soar! Leaders must fly. Godly men and husbands must fly. Virtuous women and wives must fly. Fired up youth must fly. In order to be bold prophets and Godly activists, zealous evangelists, focused pastors, anointed teachers, effective administrators, true worshippers, spirit-filled apostles, church planters and warring intercessors we must fly. If we don't fly, God's glory has no abode on earth. If we don't fly, the Kingdom of God will pale in comparison to the fascinating yet temporary, fleeting and shallow kingdoms of this world. If we don't fly, the church will not rise to its ordained spiritual and institutional heights in these last days. If we don't fly, men and women will grope for and find other sources of inspiration. If we don't fly, the devil will get the glory. If we don't fly, if we don't soar, if we don't come in the fullness of the power of the blessing of Christ then:

- The gospel witness will not expand...
- The healing of the sick will not occur...
- The restoration of the lost will not take place...
- The advance of the church will not be fulfilled in our time...
- The poor will not rise...
- The rich will not bow...
- Justice will be delayed...
- Hope will be denied and...
- Love will not abide if we don't fly!
- Our children will got to jail...
- Our brothers will go to hell (and live one too)...
- Our sisters are sure to fail...
- Our daughters will stray...
- Our sons will not stay on the Godly narrow way...
- Our homes will dismantle...
- Our communities will be in shambles...
- The drunk won't get delivered...
- The addict will keep to quiver...

For that same useless hit, and he will not quit until you, me, we, church, eagles, Fly!

CHAPTER II

The Hook-Up

LET THE CHURCH SAY AMEN

Now upon every eagle there's been a bestowal of resources God has richly granted. This unique set of resources working together function to fulfill God's planned purpose for your flight, your personal mission to fullness. Every eagle has a set of them. They were bestowed in harmony with God's creative and pre-ordained purpose at and before your appearing. They're in there. The deposit has been made. All that you need to fly is already within. But you must possess these resources and move to being possessed by them. You must possess them because it is possible for you to allow them to reside in you without grabbing hold of them. It is possible for you to have millions of dollars in your account, but if you don't know it's there and don't withdraw it to use it you have missed your blessing. You had it, but you didn't possess it. You owned it, but you didn't claim it.

Possessing these resources means agreeing with the truth that you have them. And no one can do this for you. No one can possess what's inside of you but you. Prophets can prophesy it. Others can discern its presence. God can even speak and tell you it's there. But if you don't say Amen to the truth, no flying will take place.

This Amen is an inner conviction and decision to believe what God has already done in you. It is a decision to search out the gold and diamonds secured in the vaults of your spirit. When you come to terms with how rich you really are, flying is inevitable because you cannot possess faith without faith possessing you. You cannot possess the anointing of God, that is, believe that it is upon you in an area, without the anointing of God possessing you. You know when someone has possessed God's gifts because their gifts possess them.

Consider the way of Eagles. They don't trust in the air to fly. Eagles know what and who they are, and thus they fly in the air. But the power is not in the air or in the wings. Likewise for us, our power to rise to fullness is not in our environment or in our material resources. The power is in knowing what we've got.

For the eagle, the air merely represents the environment which provides nothing but the place where they do their thing. In the process of being real to itself, the eagle transforms environment to the extent that it (air) will have to honor the flight. And eventually it will not only honor the flight, but in some cases carry the eagle to its next destination without the mighty bird having to flap a wing.

Just being a lowly little pastor with a flock of about seventy down in the armpit of the country hardly gives me credibility to speak with authority on the subject I am presenting in this book. Nevertheless, I perform this ministry task because I have come to terms with the truth that I am a man of great vision, of great faith, a birther under an apostolic anointing to plant and pioneer, a creator, a zealous voice gift practitioner, counselor, comforter, social prophet and writer. That first spin about being in the armpit merely reflects my environment. The latter description entails what I possess and what I am possessed by. But **I** had to come to terms with this truth. Maybe others had seen it. But if I didn't say Amen to it, I'd continue to walk in less than the fullness. And once I said okay to the miracle that is me, I took flight by reason of the power contained in that truth alive and flourishing in my spirit. What you possess within your spirit regarding spiritual matters is what you will be possessed by.

Never accept the descriptions about your environment as the "spin" on you, as the news about you that shapes your reality. You'll realize, and many of you already have, that there are self-appointed talking heads in the Kingdom of God who believe it their task to give the "spin" on you so as to set limitations or satisfy their addictions to control. They will control you as long as you let them. But when you decide their "spin" has no authority, they'll move on to another turkey to bake. The sad thing is until you break from believing their spin you are participating in their lie, giving it legitimacy and power.

Remember that you have your own hook-up to the news about the latest on you. You already have access to the breaking story in this season. You need no reporter, no talking head. You need no secondhand information. Your anchorman has direct access to your spirit. And His name is the Holy Ghost.

HALLELUJAH FOR THE HOOK-UP!

Possessing and being possessed by the wealth within you is predicated upon your position. You must be connected, **Hooked-Up**, completely to the resourcer who is the Holy Spirit in order to see, hear, know and understand what God has poured into you. Positioned in the Holy Ghost amid the treasury is where eagles discover their true identities and purposes. The Apostle Paul declares:

> *"The Spirit Himself bears witness with our spirit that*
> *we are the children of God, and if children then*
> *heirs — heirs of God and joint heirs with Christ ..."*
> — *Romans 8:16,17*

Let it be made clear that spiritual truth, God's communication unto us, proceeds through a man or woman's spirit and that the transmitter of the message is the Holy Spirit Himself. Your mind/consciousness does not act alone in receiving and storing God's message for you. In fact, your mind cannot act alone. Spiritual truth is sent through a spiritual medium (Holy Spirit) and deposited in a spiritual receptor (your spirit). Those in great depths of intimacy with Christ have witnessed that God deposits direction, messages or concern for people or issues within their spirits. This work of God is no magical or shady phenomena. This is not the testimony of people who are fanatics or "overly spiritual," if there is such a thing. These are people who understand that God is a Spirit and that He has formed within our make-up the means for communion and communication with Him. These people are spiritually astute enough to discern the distinctions between their spirit and their mental consciousness. And this is important because the fullness of spiritual transformation takes place in our spirits which leads to a new mind, not the other way around.

That's why our Gospel speaks of being born again as regeneration, a new birth of our spirit. Nicodemus could not understand spiritual truth with his mind because something critical had not taken place in his spirit! Know that you can lose consciousness of spiritual truth. In addition, your subconscious also is limited in what it can hold or retain. Consciousness is available but limited data in the sphere of awareness. Subconsciousness is the limited place of storage of data until called forward to consciousness. Memory is associated with ability to call certain parts of that data forward. Your spirit, however, is the storehouse of spiritual truth which when poured in shakes the very ground of every facet of your being. Your spirit has one orientation and purpose, communication and communion with God. Conversely, you can choose to be either carnally or spiritually minded. This is why Nicodemus was in the midst of spiritual truth but received nothing. His spirit was not hooked up to the Holy Spirit who reveals spiritual truth *(John 3:1-9)*. In fact, His spirit was not even made alive to Christ. The Master Teacher, the Author and Finisher of our faith, spoke spiritual truth to a man who left confused because he only invested his consciousness and not his spirit. There ought to be some ground-shaking communication in your spirit because it is the seat of the fullness of transformation. You must have more than Jesus on your mind; you must have the ground-shaking truth about His deposit in your spirit.

Now we are more blessed than Nicodemus ever was, even though he had an encounter with our Lord face to face in the flesh. If you are reading this book, you're probably already a Believer who has the Holy Spirit living inside of you which gives you a benefit he didn't have. Your task on the way to flight is to strengthen your hook-up so that you don't miss the spiritual truth God wants to elevate you with! This is why the Holy Spirit is called the Spirit of Truth and why Christ proclaims the Holy Spirit will lead us into all truth. The Holy Spirit enables us to see divine truth about ourselves which under normal circumstances or conditions we are not able to see.

But hold it. There's more, exceedingly more. It is equally true that the Holy Spirit is released to do a work of fullness in as much as we engage holy practices such as prayer, fasting and worship. Here I am not talking about a few words on the run or merely doing your ritual hour and a half time on Sundays.

I'm speaking about a heart stretched out toward God in adoration and desperation that pours over into your lifestyle. I'm speaking of a disciplined prayer life inspired by the fact that you know you need Him more than food, water and air, so that He's the first thing you reach for in the morning, the last thing you reach for at night and everything you reach for in between. I'm talking about blood stain sacrifice where you give up stuff for Him so that you can discover that His glory can't even be compared to the pain of you letting go of the stuff you thought was all that. What releases the Holy Ghost in the fullness of power is the arrival at the increasing level of stuff you can live without. For this condition of being without builds strength of spirit, molds character and creates pathways for God's power and blessing.

Like an abundance of African American men who grew up and still grow up in contemporary urban U.S. cities, I did not have the benefit of my father's presence growing up. While this has, I believe, stunted me in some ways, it has built character, resolve and determination; a kind of tenacity and will to overcome. But I believe that's the sub-plot. The real story is the woman who was responsible for pouring those traits within me without the help of a man to do so. There may not be a more difficult task than a woman trying to develop and teach a young boy in hostile urban America how to be a man. And while I turned out far from perfect, I am also far from destruction and progressing from glory to glory. Momma did it without daddy! And this is the testimony. It is not that I had no father, but that she had the strength, will, resolve and tenacity to make me who I am. She became father. She became what I needed. She unclothed herself and took on the form of a man! Sounds like Jesus stuff to me! But this challenge was created within the context of doing without what she needed. There are millions like her whose witness to Christ plays itself out within the context of being what's needed in the face of performing without. To all the mothers like mine in the world who have taken on the form of man and shown forth the Christ witness, I say Hallelujah to God.

I am reminded of the recently released film produced and directed by Denzel Washington titled *Antwone Fisher*. It is based on the true story of a young African-American urban kid who arrives safely to manhood without his mother and father. It weaves the details of the abuses he suffered and the process of his triumphant arrival at the discovery of his biological parents who abandoned him. Simultaneously, he found courage to confront religious foster parents who abused him. Underlying this central narrative is his counselor played by Washington who has died emotionally due to having to live without a son (his wife cannot conceive). Both Fisher and Washington are reborn and made better for their journeys, as they find each other on the road to their healing. But a critical test for both of their lives is not necessarily what they have to deal with. Really it's what they have to deal without.

Our spiritual lives carry this kind of challenge. Our commitment to God often is measured by what we are willing and capable of doing without. The popular "prosperity gospel" movement which is pervasive within American Christendom highlights a curious tension between our status as joint heirs with Christ (meaning we are to be prosperous in all things) and God's obvious work of spiritual formation which often takes place as we are without.

In no way do I intend to ordain poverty. The transformation of our socio-economic systems into just, equitable and provisional structures is the ongoing concern for the biblically prophetic. But we do honestly assess the value of void in the spiritual formation toward wholeness and how Jesus the Master Discipler teaches us disciples that conditions of void can measure what you're made of. And sometimes they remain when or until God's gets the greatest glory.

Jesus went without a place to lay His head. He went without one disciple really understanding the fullness of who He was. And when Peter was graced with a glimpse of the real Jesus, it was not long afterward that he fled to the enemy when the cross loomed large. Jesus went without support from His hometown Nazarenes who tried to push Him off a cliff. He went without acceptance from His Jewish community who eventually had Him hanged on a tree. He went without Joseph's lifelong fatherly companionship and without the continual crowds to affirm His person rather than His miracles. Even on the cross He went without the comfort He wanted from His heavenly Father, for He cried out in the despair of abandonment and isolation as He hung nailed to that tree. But what is increasingly clear is that the one thing that never left and that maintained Him through all the storms and adversities was the Hook-Up!!! And when the Hook-Up was threatened, He knew what to do to preserve it as He cried to the Father,

> *"...into thy hands I commend my spirit."*
> — *Luke 23:46*

He was crucified. But the devil couldn't touch His Hook-Up, His spirit, His communion and communication with his God, the instrument through which the power of the resurrection would flow.

So no matter what you may be going through right now, whatever you do or don't do, don't let it mess with your Hook-Up! Don't allow a situation to occur when God wants to dial you up and raise you up but finds that your line has been disconnected and is temporarily out of service. Maintain your Hook-Up! Worship! Pray! Fast! Now! Because you are too gifted, too anointed and too beautiful to go out like that! Can't you see that?

DO YOU SEE WHAT I SEE?!!!

A most awesome way that God makes ground-shaking truth an unshakable reality in our lives is through visions and dreams. Both of these were highly used by God in the biblical revelation in order to uncover for His people His purposes and plans. And one need not be some identified mystic or appointed saint in order to be the beneficiary of visions and dreams. All you need is, you guessed it, the Hook-Up! Who are mystics except those who respond to the imperative to "walk in the Spirit"? And who are the saints except everyone everywhere who calls on the Name of the Lord and who are called by His Name? In this age we have surrendered the God-centered, Spirit-drenched life and lifestyle to the priests, nuns, bishops, prophets and apostles. While we require them to walk in the Spirit, we are quite content to be running in the flesh, stopping in on the mighty flow of God every now and then, only to leave commenting on the activity of the power of God in somebody else. Aren't you tired of talking? Don't you want to be the one somebody's talking about? Aren't you tired of being part of that group who specializes in standing on the outside looking in. Aren't you tired of wondering what's wrong with you as you ponder, in the midst of God's move, why you ain't got it like that? Well, then, hook it up!

I remember when God started showing me He wanted to hook me up. I was a senior at William Jewell College, a small but highly touted liberal arts college just outside Kansas City. As I approached my senior year, I began to think about what I would do next. I sat down in my dorm room in April of 1986 to reflect on my future. I took a pen and pad out and began to write options on a piece of paper. The first option I wrote was graduate school. The second option I wrote was the Armed Forces. The third option I wrote was corporate America. Then there was a strange fourth option I wrote down. It was the monastery. The monastery! Why on earth would a 22-year-old African-American young man from the ghetto of Kansas City with a bachelor's degree, living a bachelor's dream (if you know what I mean), with a gangster dad in jail as my role model even be thinking about living a monastic life? What would cause me to think of such a thing? I understand now that there was nothing in my consciousness that caused such a reflection. I'd never been to a monastery. I knew no monks. I was not even aware of how you become one. Even now I still must go to the dictionary to spell it correctly. I had no mental, conscious or subconscious frame of reference. Let's be real. Black kids don't grow up in contemporary urban America longing to be monks. But what I did have was an imprint upon my spirit. This imprint was pressed one Sunday morning ten years earlier as I kneeled to pray in Mass at the age of twelve. The Spirit of the Lord came over me as I knelt with my mamma by my side. And I felt an overwhelming warmth and power causing me to shake and weep as I prayed and sought the Lord's attention to my concerns. Little did I know it then, but my spirit had been shaken. A deposit had been made. I know now that my monastic forays were only an extension of the shaking that took place in worship and prayer as I knelt ten years earlier. Yeah, He shook me up to hook me up. And now time was approaching for the hook. I realize now that I'm not called to be a monk, but I am called to a monk's devotion. I'm not called to be a monk, but I am called to a monk's consecration. I'm not called to the monastery, but I am called to take the holiness of the monastic life to the world. It was in this instant in this dorm room that God began to give me His vision for my life. But the shaking, the deposit, the imprint upon my spirit had taken place long ago.

We must always remember that God shakes us, touching our spirit to show us vision that prompts human response, spiritual resolve and commitment to mission. Spiritual ecstasy without divine enlightenment is nothing more than self-fulfillment. Divine encounter without spiritual formation and growth in purpose is merely religious fornication. When is the last time you had a divine encounter? But more importantly, what did He show you in the depths of your spirit that leaves you all shook up and ready to fly?

But God wasn't finished with me. There was more of me that remained to be seen. In fact, vision is about God turning you on to the stuff he sees about your future in Him. Now know that you can begin to receive the hook-up and still be, in some way, on lock-down. It is true that the hook-up is created to free people from being locked down by the entrapments and strongholds of the opposition.

As unbelievable as it may seem, some of the most powerful, anointed and acclaimed folks in public can be some of the most hampered, weak and locked-down folks in private. I cannot count the number of awards I received during my five-year stay pursuing my bachelor's degree. I was a star point guard and captain in basketball, president of the Black Students' Association, a residential assistant with student affairs and received numerous awards for character, leadership, service and popularity contests. My strength in public was awesome. Nevertheless, there remained serious flaws in me which resulted from the sense of abandonment I felt from my father, sexual abuse I endured as a child from older female neighbors, and the environment of drugs and alcohol I was exposed to in the "hood." Thus I shined by day. But my light sometimes dimmed by night.

I began to experiment with marijuana, attempting to escape the pressures of my need to lead the collegial starship. Once I broke away with a couple of others to relish in my status, position and awards, knowing that kids from where I come don't ordinarily walk where I was walking or do what I was doing. So "gittin' high" and reflecting on how high I had come in achievement became a temptation. This particular night in April was one of those nights. It was about two weeks after the monastic reflection. I picked up a textbook to review some material for an exam, and while reading I suddenly had a mind to read the Bible. It was not common for me to pick up the Bible and read it. I had no disciplined life of prayer or worship whatsoever. Yet I had a mind to pick up a Bible. I grabbed hold of Grandma's old Bible she gave me when she died a few years earlier and somehow came to the Gospel of John. Though my mind was cloudy, the hook-up would not wait any longer, and

I found myself reading these words of Jesus:

"...I am the bread of life.
He who comes to me shall never hunger,
and he who believes in me
shall never thirst."
— John 6:35

These words so shook me that I've never been the same. Anything shaken with enough strength will break, even the hardest of things. Nicknamed Stoney, I had developed the character and personality in the hood of being cool, emotionless and unaffected by people and events. This night, however, Stoney left. And the wings of someone who I was beginning to see emerged in an instant. Upon reading this text, I went to the marijuana pouch, took my stash to the toilet, flushed it down and have not returned to it since. I graduated the next month in May. But the real matriculation took place that night.

This has been a lesson for me in ministry. Everybody needs healing in one way or another. Some of the most charismatic, committed and critically acclaimed folks within the Kingdom and outside of it are the most in need. Never think that people who do big things somehow don't still need God to do big things in them.

I call to your attention the strong man Samson of the Old Testament who defeated the enemy armies with the power of an anointing from God that no opposition could stand against *(Judges 16)*. His power surpassed the realistic expectations of both His friends and foes. But unlike other battles in the Old

Testament, God actually gave Samson the physical strength to defeat enemies. With David, Jehoshaphat and the Mosaic narratives, there is a mysterious sense of God intervening in the battles giving a weak Judah or Israelite army the victory by fighting the battle Himself.

In the Samson narratives the picture carries a different nuance. There is in Samson this picture of a man whose physical strength is increased by virtue of the anointing of God upon him. With David, God intervenes for the underdog. With Samson God gives him this supernatural power to do it himself. But as strong as he was by day, he was weak in the knees at night. For still, there was a woman named Delilah who possessed the power to put Samson in lock-down in the secret and hidden realities of his existence. And his condition was so bad that it impacted his ability to work for God in the day because that which was the key to his strength was disposable to him in his weakness. He was willing to give up his locks to suffer lock-down. Ultimately this was an indication of the weakness of his worship. In Samson's assessment God and His strength proved unworthy to suffer the blood stain of the loss of Delilah. In that sense there is no real separation from what we do in the day and what we do in the night. But nor is there any real separation from our praise on Sunday and our choices Monday through Saturday. They grow from the same ground upon which we assess His worthiness.

And if God is not worthy enough to be obeyed on Monday, no level of passion or vigor of shout we give on Sunday can prove Him Lord of our lives or anybody else's. In our disobedience we withhold the sacrifice. Show me your blood stain? Therein is your worship.

Those of us still on lock-down can be warned that it will affect everything else we do. But we also can be assured that the key to our deliverance is in the house. His name is Jesus and the hook-up is available. But you must answer: What or who is your Delilah?

Vision is when God shows you she (Delilah) doesn't fit in His picture for you and gives you a divine view of what does. God is trying to show you what He sees when He looks at you. He is simply asking: "Do you see what I see?"

Visions and dreams are the stuff of the future, the substance of God's will and purpose for our lives and the church seen and exposed to our spirits. John's litany of revelatory visions in the apocalyptic text is that which was given to him as he was "in the Spirit on the Lord's Day" *(Revelation 1:10)*. As we have established, anything given by the Holy Spirit is transmitted through and received by our spirit.

God's announcement through Joel regarding visions and dreams are a result of an outpouring and inworking of the Holy Spirit *(Joel 2:28)*. Visions and dreams are inseparable from this dynamic.

When visions and dreams are revealed (shown), divine purpose is conceived. When visions and dreams are pursued, divine purpose is born. When visions and dreams are nurtured, divine purpose grows and matures. When visions and dreams are solidified, divine purpose is fully established.

Visions and dreams provide the intangible picture of what

God wants to see tangibly manifest in the activity and affairs of His people.

Visions and dreams are the specific blueprint for the handiwork of God as His Kingdom advances and expands.

Visions and dreams are given by God to the spirits of leaders by the Holy Spirit because it is leadership that holds the ministry task of administration and strategy to ensure the blue print becomes structural, operational and functional to touch the lives of people that the Lion of Judah might receive praise through the healing and restoration of people.

Visions and dreams are by nature prophetic because they apply divine pressure upon us and this current existential reality to be transformed into the image and will of God. For when we are shown divine picture we are burdened to be changed and to become change agents for the cause of the Kingdom.

Eagles are folks who have been graced by God to have seen the otherwise hidden picture of God's blessed purpose for their lives. Eagles, before you see them flying, had already seen themselves in flight before they mounted. For you see, visions and dreams aid tremendously in flight. Your predominant, prevailing picture of who you are is what you will ultimately become. Visions and dreams work to ensure that your prevailing picture is in harmony with God's.

Now a warning: What you see may shock you. Likewise, others probably will not understand you when you begin your mount. But do not let this stop you. You must believe what you see. Hallelujah! And if what you see is not unbelievable, you haven't been with God!

The man or woman under the anointing stirred to activation of their spiritual gifts is capable of flying. The woman acutely and confidently aware of her intangible spiritual attributes is about to mount. The man at peace and empowered by past mistakes and historical failures is armed for victory. And the one who caps all these with Holy Ghost shown vision and dreams can't help but fly. You're rich. If you don't know, now you know!!!

CHAPTER III

Cooped Up and Ready to Fly

YOUR DAY IN THE COOP

Every eagle really does have its day in the coop, that caged and bound area where chickens await to be devoured. Each of us has or will experience being in places, surroundings, activities or among people which do not harmonize with the height and dimensions of our destiny. Coops are places that no longer, or never did, serve purpose in where you are going. Nor do they aid in the process of living out who you are. Becoming one with God's vision for you often means becoming separated from what once were comfortable people or places. Many men and women in the Bible flew the coop to their greater destinies in God.

Noah flew the coop of sin and judgment to safety and restoration. Abraham flew the coop of Ur and its dead end to the land of promise and blessing. Joseph flew the coop of pithood in the desert to princehood in Egypt. Israel the nation, named after Joseph's daddy, flew the coop of Egypt to the fertile ground of Canaan. David flew the coop of sheeptending to the battle against Goliath. Nehemiah flew the coop of Babylon to rebuilding the wall of Jerusalem. Job flew the coop of despair and pity to the high ground of patience and hope. Jonah flew the coop of the belly of a big fish to the mission field of Nineveh. Paul flew the coop of the Pharisees' doctrine to the bright glory of apostleship.

Coops are places, whether emotional, physical, mental or

spiritual, which no longer serve purpose in where you're going or the God process of living out who you are as an eagle. The fact is, eagles fly! And we know deep in our spirits when we are and when we are not. Likewise, we know those things that keep us from flying or at least provide no room or inspiration to. We know our coops.

Cooped-up eagles are everywhere. Some of them are in our nation's prisons. Some of them are in abusive relationships. Some of them are in crowded homeless shelters. Others are addicted to alcohol or drugs. Others sell their bodies for money in exchange for sexual pleasures. Others sell their souls in corporate enterprise which exploits the poor in exchange for wealth and power. Some others live dormant lives in a mundane and meaningless existence without vigor, vibrance or vitality. They rise and fall with the sun every day but never see or experience the light and glow of God break upon their lives. Still others are in churches sitting in pews, standing at pulpits, wearing choir robes, serving within the Kingdom, yet cooped up. They fail to walk in the fullness of the power of the blessing of God which is what it means to fly. They're eagles. They're just cooped up.

Where's your coop? What's his name? What does she do that sends you there? About how long does it preoccupy you a day, a week, a month, a year? And where could you be now if you hadn't been cooped up?

When are you going to release yourself from the coops God has already delivered you from? When are you going to loose yourself from people, places and things which do not inspire you nor aspire to fly themselves? Stop hanging out with spiritual flunkies who help

to cage you in and dry you out! For you see, there is human involvement in preparation for your flight.

In the scriptures when Christ freed the man to ascend to his created purpose of fullness, He did so by giving divine command: "Loose him and let him go." *(John 11:44)* It is always divine command which authorizes flight. But human hands untie and unravel the bands. By the power vested in me as God's prophet, I proclaim the divine command of "fullness" God has spoken and authorized in your life! Now, untie yourself. Do it now because the longer you're in the coop, the greater your chances of staying there. That's because you can't continue in the coop without the coop increasing in you. Every moment you spend in the coop, the coop spends solidifying its space and place in you. Untie yourself! The devil is defeated! You are authorized for take-off!

Part of what sets chickens and eagles apart is that eagles have heard the divine command spoken prophetically into their spirits. It has been spoken so powerfully that we keep hearing it over and over again. This is why the psalmist declares,

> *"Once hath he spoken it,*
> *Twice have I heard it,*
> *That power belongs to God."*
> *— Psalm 62:11*

The reality of flying, of operating in the fullness of the power and blessing of God, is a haunting echo reverberating over and over again rendering the spirit of one restless until fullness has way. For you see, God didn't even make chickens, not in the spirit realm. Every man or woman born again and yet not walking in the fullness (or at least harassed by the vision of it) has not heard the divine command. It comes with power, strong and enforcing, yet gentle and with grace.

Don't be deceived. You ain't no chicken. You're just cooped up. But now divine command has come, and there's plenty of room in the skies. In fact, God tends to place certain people in areas where the barns are crowded and the skies are empty. And when the divine command is heard and the eagle in you begins to mount, you will be bothered by this unbalanced ratio. You'll know when it's time to mount because you will begin to ask yourself: why so much pecking and so little flying? You're not meant to be cooped up forever. God intended it to be temporary. It's just for a season. And that season lasts long enough for God to show other people what He's able to do. It is shown as He handles His business through you. As you walk in the fullness, somebody is going to catch a vision of themselves for themselves. Suddenly they see themselves out of their own coop but it was aided by you walking in the fullness. God has set some people in coops just so their rise can be noted, documented and seen. You're in the coop to rise. Hallelujah! That's why you're there. You're cooped up to mount up.

Christ knew this in His own journey. He said repeatedly to His disciples that He would suffer the cross and spend time in the gallows of death's chambers. But he never stated this without stating also in the same breath that He would rise on the third day. Note that His stay in the chambers of hell had long-term divine purpose but short-term, temporary status. There came a time when the purpose was completed. And when that moment came there was no question it was time to mount up. After long-term purpose was completed, so was His stay in the grave. Any length of time in the grave beyond that pre-ordained third day would have meant that our Lord was cooped up. And we don't serve a cooped-up Jesus, we serve a raised-up one. When you go beyond your time in a particular condition, you're cooped up. Sometimes God will allow you a season in the chambers not as your end, but instead to serve His ends! If His ends have been served and you're still where you were, then you're cooped up. Go tell everybody you're cooped up with your time is up and ask them if they want to go with you.

You see, it is not all the time that coops are necessarily "bad places." Often they're just past places which helped to prepare you to mount. When you develop the spiritual audacity and courageous tenacity to mount up to your higher purpose, you transform that coop into a nest. In effect, it was the place that held you until you were ready to take flight.

Coops hem you in. Nests launch you out. Coops debilitate you. Nests facilitate you. Coops devour your spirit. Nests empower your spirit. Coops hold you until you die. Nests feed you until you fly.

YOU ARE CLEARED FOR TAKE-OFF

Of all the Old Testament prophets, Elijah stands out as one who assuredly walked in the fullness of the power of God. His lifestyle, reputation and mission actions speak clearly and plainly to such. Christ Himself said that no prophet was greater than John the Baptist due to his place as forerunner. The biblical testimony is that John the Baptist came in the spirit and power of Elijah. Well, what is the spirit and power of Elijah? And what does it have to do with fullness? If Jesus is right (and I tend to believe Him), then John the Baptist was the greatest prophet/preacher ever. And if John the Baptist came in the spirit and power of Elijah, it behooves us to know what the spirit and power of Elijah is.

Well, firstly we know the outcomes of the spirit and power of Elijah. These outcomes flowed through the ministry of John the Baptist. These outcomes included: 1) the act of proclaiming an uncompromising message no matter what the consequences; 2) demonstrating unusual and awesome power to reach the inner core of men's hearts; 3) the uncanny ability to both usher in a New Dimension of spirituality and faith for a new age; and 4) reveal that New Dimension so that all would be able to share in identifying Him as He is ushered in. Of course, that New Dimension who was to be revealed and identified was Christ Himself.

These four outcomes were evident in the life of John the Baptist. His ability to usher in the New Dimension and identify Him is apparent in both his stated purpose as forerunner to Jesus and the first and chief identifier of Jesus as the Christ. John the Baptist is adamant in the text that there is One who is coming after him who is greater than him. And John is at least as equally zealous in His identification of this New Dimension as He appears in the flesh as the saving Son of God. Most everyone else is offended, shocked, angered or amused at the notion of Jesus being the Messiah. John the Baptist, having never seen or heard the Master do or say anything, cried out at the moment of Jesus' mere arrival, "Behold the Lamb of God who takes away the sins of the world" *(John 1:29)*. Utterly uncanny, John the Baptist reveals Grace and Truth with absolutely no evidence at all except spiritual sensitivities, which would be the ensuing trademark and requirement for those who would ultimately believe on His name.

Along with uncanny spiritual sensitivities toward revelation of God's fresh move was John the Baptist's unusual and extraordinary access to reach the core of men's hearts. What is not mentioned in detail but clearly explicit in the text is that John the Baptist had sparked a spiritual revival in Galilee. The Bible is clear that his ministry baptized many and that he had disciples who followed and aided him in the advance of his cause. The multitude of individuals, who were rebuffed rather than restored by the exclusionary and empty religion of the first century spiritual leadership, were touched at the core of their hearts by that which flowed from John the Baptist. People responded from their hearts with submission to a message and vision of repentance, personal moral renewal and a beloved community marked by social provision. This preacher touched hearts.

A fourth outcome of the spirit and power of Elijah was the proclamation of uncompromising word. Clearly evident in his ministry was his refusal to negotiate with those who opposed his message. Thus, this crying voice was jailed and ultimately executed for no other reason than he would not change God's message. If he would change it he could live. But he refused. In this sense, the concerns of the Kingdom of God, in John's mind, outweighed even his own life. God's message was nonnegotiable. Indeed, these were powerful outcomes. They were produced by the "spirit and power of Elijah" operative within John the Baptist. Yet, there is still more to be seen. For the question becomes: how or in what context does such spirit and power, such fullness if you will, birth and flourish? One answer is the womb of isolation!

Consider that nearly one thousand years elapsed between the appearance of Elijah and John the Baptist. But they appeared under the same fullness of spirit and power and ironically, out from the same remote wilderness of isolation. Often those fresh out of the obscurity of isolation and repose arrive operating under fullness. This divine sequence must be honored if fullness is to have way. We are cleared for take-off by God, the flight commander, inasmuch as we have spent some significant time in isolation having had some significant work done in us. This "doing time" does not perfect us, but prepares us for the imperfection we are about to encounter in and around us. Nor does this "doing time" end our preparation; it only signals the end of that stage of preparation which only isolation can perfect. Many who were mighty instruments in the hand of God spent time in the matrix of isolation which prepared them for ultimate launch to new spiritual heights, vision and mission. Public demonstrations of power are directly connected to private practices of piety, devotion and single hearted worship.

For the Apostle Paul it was nearly a twenty-year stay in the Arabian Desert. For Moses it was tending sheep on the backside of Mount Sinai in the remote area of Midian. For John, the Gospel writer and revelator, it was exiled alone on the Island of Patmos. For Elijah it was the deserted countryside of dried-up brooks, mysterious ravens, poor widows and starving children. For John the Baptist it was the wilderness of Judea. For our Christ it was isolated stints in far-off places like Tyre or the Garden of Gethsemane.

It seems that "out of nowhere," out of the matrix of isolation and aloneness, God prepares the hearts and spirits of His servants as they emerge consumed by spiritual fire that rages within once one has rested in the bosom of the Father. This isolation helped produce in John the Baptist a fire, a fullness, that entanglements with the world's affairs, concerns and desires can choke or quench. John the Baptist was an unquenched voice untouched by the world's norms. And this is a prime issue in fullness. God's move is sometimes predicated by somebody emerging to a new city, church, neighborhood or family out from their previous hidden place. I like to call these folks originals. They are not stained or numbed by the context in which they minister and live out their purpose. They transform, alter and impact that context.

You see, radical change toward the Kingdom of God is facilitated by folks fully unlike that which they are called to. The 120-plus in the upper room were told by Jesus to stay in isolation until they were filled with something wholly unlike anything in the world. Then, they were cleared for take-off. Out from the isolation they came one day, and the world has not been the same since.

Someone who is reading this little book is grieving from the loss of friends or the transition to a new ministry. Someone has broken off old relationships in search of new power. Someone right now is heartbroken and disillusioned at what appears to be loss of stuff around you when in reality this is God's time to move in you like never before. Just maybe for somebody reading this, everything has changed and just about everybody's gone. If you look around and there's nobody left except you and God, well, shout Hallelujah! God may be telling you, *"It's My Turn Now!!!"*

WHEN COOPS TURN INTO NESTS

One of the most telling events which take place in the life of Elijah is his final act recorded in *2 Kings, chapter 2*. This final act was to strike the Jordan with his mantle which was the symbol of his power, personality and authority. At the striking of the Jordan, the waters divided. This act, witnessed by his understudy Elisha, was the final act of many in the ministry of one consumed by the fullness. His successor, Elisha, had only one request:

"Please let a double portion of your spirit be upon me."
— **2 Kings 2:9**

Note the desire these words speak to. It is a desire to walk in a power no less than, and in fact, exceeding his mentor. It is a desire for peak spiritual performance. It is a desire for optimum spiritual power. But Elisha could never have envisioned such exceeding greatness without his mentor flowing in the fullness. Elisha had documented the fullness within his mentor, and now the season for him to fly the coop of understudy to the skies of lead prophet and messenger was present. This young upstart now has a vision of an elevated purpose. By seeing Elijah, he now sees himself in a new light. Operating as Elijah's understudy was not a bad place; it was just a past place which helped to prepare him for his flight.

When where you are is no longer in harmony with your purpose and the process of living out who you are becoming as an eagle, then you are cooped up. When you develop the spiritual audacity and courageous tenacity to mount up to your higher purpose, you transform that coop into a nest. In effect, it was the place that fed you until you were ready to take flight.

Who's your Elijah? Where's the place you witness fullness? When do you have opportunities to see, experience and know folks who light your fire because they give you a glimpse of where you're going in God?

THE ORIGINAL

Well, if you have no Elijah, no place to witness fullness and no opportunity to dwell with somebody who knows soaring, don't fret. Maybe you're just one of those oddly zealous and peculiar folks for whom there is no clear model to follow and no mold to pattern yourself after. Perhaps you've never considered it before, but I raise it for you today. Who did Elijah have to pattern his life and ministry after? The answer is no one.

Elijah was one of those about whom we can say there existed none like him before. But wonderfully so, Elijah's most profound offering could be that he depended upon no external clues for how he would proceed and fulfill God's purposes. Strangely, he had no one like himself to follow. Elijah represents God's creative and artistic Spirit in concert with power to produce originals for a fading, fledgling world. Elijah had no manual, no mentor and no model. Nobody was present to give him clear definition of who he was becoming and what he had to offer up for God. This was by design, for only a prophet formed in isolation could be used to alter the stiff realities of the day. He only had folks in the school of the prophets who were looking to him for clarity. This prophet was God's invention for the times. Sometimes when God's handiwork is being crafted we have to read and observe the work itself. And sometimes that work is us.

It is quite possible that you are an Elijah, purposed for

**such awesome and unique deeds and ways that there exists
no one around you who is flowing in such a way that is
harmonious to who you are becoming.
You may very well have to cease and desist your
search for those who would reinforce God's creative work
which is you, and just proceed to write your own manual.
You may just be an original!**

Never allow the obscurity around you to cloud the sharp
and succinct purpose God has deposited within you. If there
isn't a trail, then blaze one. And let your unwavering devotion
to God and His purposes in your life pave the way. Your legitimacy is derived from honoring your authentic self. Your path
is charted by your relentless dreams and visions. If there's
nobody around who embodies the power and personality of
your destiny, who can make a difference in your flight, then
you be the difference. Be an original!

God has placed some people in cities, churches, denominations, organizations, ministries or even eras where they have to
rely more on their own inner strength than most other people.
The difference in the plight, and therefore flight, of these folks
lies within them rather than in their relationships with those
around them. The difference for the people of God is always
within. The power and life force to fly is witnessed by what
comes flowing out from within us. This is why Jesus said of
those who believe in Him, "… out of your heart shall flow
rivers of living water." *(John 7:37)*. He was referencing that the
spiritual power and life force He would bestow would be an
indwelling force that would shape, mold, alter and transform
the outer world. The difference is within you.

When you develop the spiritual tenacity to mount up to

your higher purpose, you transform the coop you have been held in to a nest you were being nurtured in. Whatever happened while you were there, good or bad, has helped to shape you for this moment when you are deciding now that you are going to soar. Count it all joy. Let God work it together for the good and get to flying. And the moment you make that decision, you have just transformed what was a debilitating coop into a nurturing nest that provided some of the substance for your launch. What made the difference? You did! Where was the difference? Inside of you!

This truth is illustrated over and over in the life of Jesus. The Savior had to always depend upon this inner knowledge and strength in spite of hostile, contrary or unfavorable outer forces that sought to deny, counter or oppose Him.

His very conception and birth gives testimony to this. There is no logical reason why Gabriel, the lofty and esteemed messenger, would term lowly Mary as royalty with the greeting of "Hail" except that she carried within her the One, the seed of immortality, who would make the difference for the entire world.

There can be no logical explanation why John the Baptist would leap in the womb at that same Mary's appearance except that he discerned the presence of the Savior who would emerge from within her.

Why would Magi bring frankincense, gold and myrrh to give as they fall in worship of a baby born in a barn and out of wedlock except within that newborn flowed the future shed blood that would save throughout eternity.

The last time I checked my Bible it assured me that the same anointing that rested upon Him rests upon us and that we are seated with Him in heavenly places.

So ask yourself why demons tremble at the activity of you travailing in prayer, fear at the sight of you fasting, panic when you practice perseverance, try to interfere when you intercede, return after you have rebuked and resisted, bow out after you have bowed down to God, accept their defeat after you accept your victory? I'll tell you why. Because the fullness of the blessing of the power of the Christ dwells within you!

Why on earth would God send His only begotten Son, His beloved, to hang and suffer and die on a tree in humiliation and pain unless from Heaven He saw within you the image of Himself. Beyond your failings, your weaknesses and your short-comings, your true self, He did see and did decree that you, eagle, were worth dying for. Now in

Jesus' name let us decree and live out that He is worth fly-ing for. Go tell somebody you were all cooped up, but right now you're ready to fly!

CHAPTER IV

The Point of No Return

THE WAY OF AN EAGLE

The title and theme of this book is inspired by the confession of Solomon in the wisdom literature of the bible. Amid all the wise counsel of teachings, axioms and sayings, he makes what could be considered a surprising claim. He declares something he does not know. There are four things which, for him, are in this category of the unknown or the "too wonderful" (out of his realm of understanding). The first of them on the list is where we get our title and theme. He writes:

> *"There are three things which*
> *are too wonderful for me,*
> *Yes, four which I do not understand:*
> *The way of an eagle in the air..."*
> — *Proverbs 30:19*

We have taken this saying and used it as a metaphor to our spiritual lives in Christ, believing there is a spiritual state and manner of operation that the Apostle Paul termed "fullness." We envision that this spiritual state and mode of operation of "fullness" is akin to the wonder, power, awe and beauty of an eagle in the air.

Like Solomon, in wonder of the "way" of an eagle soaring, there are multitudes of us who wonder during the valleys of our spiritual journey if it is possible to live out the victorious, purpose-filled life we know and imagine. And furthermore, if it is possible, what is the way? Here we call you to find comfort in knowing that there is a way. But not only that, we call you to be encouraged that the "way" is attainable, accessible and available. We need not grope in darkness for the "way" to a spiritual life of wonder, awe, power and purpose in Christ. It is the will of the Lord to both show and give it to us. Our task is to seek out the revelation that will ultimately cause us to fly. This little book, in its humblest of ways, seeks to contribute to that body of revelation. It attempts to bolster the faith of the people of God to believe in the spiritual rewards God has already bestowed. But also it attempts to birth and nurture a reality in us all that no matter what we may be going through the rewards given by God are still able to be obtained from God. In spite of the mistakes you've made, the lateness of the hour, the opportunities missed, or the wrong decisions made, the spiritual gifts and callings of God remain.

Hear the Apostle Paul speaking within the context of Israel's gift and calling of being a holy nation operating as witness to Yahweh. Paul's message is an overwhelming, often overlooked one, which uncovers the tremendous power of God's love and commitment to those he chooses. His words are clear and unmistakable.

"The gifts and callings of God are irrevocable."
— Romans 11:29

We are reminded by scripture that God is not a mere mortal who dishonors truth or lies, because He is truth. We are also reminded that nor is He the offspring of mortals prone to mistakes. His plans and purposes are perfect and need no modification.

And because you have been chosen in His pre-ordained plans to receive the rich heritage of God's spiritual gifts and calling, as long as you've got breath remaining in your flesh, you've got opportunity to show up at Daddy's house to receive your inheritance. The door is not shut on you. The banquet is not over. The table is still spread. Your inheritance is still waiting. And Daddy's still home.

Don't you want to know the way of an eagle? Don't you want to know what you're missing? Don't you want to go in God where you have not gone but are destined to in this season? Don't you want it all? I don't know about you, but I want it all! So, if you are reading this book right now, you've got the right God. The God of our Lord and Savior Jesus Christ will not leave you hanging and will not let you down. He is God alone, and there is no other God. But to take spiritual flight with awe, power and wonder, we must arrive at and take the right road. That road we call The Point of No Return. It is a road you must arrive at if you're going to fly, if fullness is going to have way.

When God graces you to finally arrive at that new position of revelation about soaring, you will become so focused and tunnel-visioned that this road we call The Point of No Return is all you want to see and a life of fullness is all you'll want to live.

But beware that this road, The Point of No Return, is a less traveled road. Not everyone who forsakes themselves to pursue the greater purposes of God does so with permanency. According to Jesus, most will not endure the spiritual journey which leads to that place of spiritual height we long for. Consequently, their leaving is inevitable. On the other hand, the road which leads to that peculiar life of spiritual height and depth is traveled by fewer. A man or woman's destiny with God shall be in large part determined by which road is chosen.

Jesus warned His disciples about this spiritual truth concerning roads. His saying advised that wide is the road that leads to destruction and narrow is the road that leads to life. The lesson is about selecting Him, the source of all life. Yet, it is also about selecting Him daily as the source for a peculiar quality of life. He counsels that the higher and harder the way, the fewer the travelers. Don't be surprised that as you ascend you become seen by more folks, but are actually known by fewer. This is because the higher you go, the fewer there are who have withstood the pull of mediocrity.

There are an estimated 8 million birds in Arizona. Only 81,000 are eagles, approximately less than 1 percent. The wildlife authorities tell us that the number of eagles has been on a steady decline for years, and no one really knows exactly why. They are considered both rare and in danger of becoming extinct. But we are told the problem is not in the birth rate. The problem is in the mortality rate. Eagles did not decrease in mating. Eaglets that were hatched found greater challenges making it to maturity. I believe that's the core issue with us. We find such hostility, opposition and contrary winds so early that we are overwhelmed and taken from the skies; but not because we couldn't hold on. Instead, because we didn't.

This is why the Point of No Return is so important. God is going to allow or deal a measure of contrary winds that push the limits of our faith and fortitude. We can only handle the push if we've reached the point, this road we call The

Point of No Return.

A major question for you is which road are you on, because being on the right road guarantees, yes, guarantees flight. We learn that God, out of His love and sovereignty, willingly surrenders Himself faithful to our unyielding strivings. If you're on the right road, you'll get to the destination … guaranteed!

THE POWER OF YOUR FLIPSIDE

Jacob's life is a testimony to this lesson. This Old Testament patriarch was familiar with this road we call The Point of No Return. I recognize that it is odd to point to Jacob as a model of spiritual flight. Indeed, most who think of Jacob refer to him as a model of what we should not be like. But I contend that the Joseph's and Naomi's of the Bible who were known for their uprightness, though models of righteousness, are not where many of us start. Jacob is raw and he's real. The Bible gives us a full picture of his transformation from start to finish. I dare say most of us don't start out like Joseph. We don't know Naomi's journey of transformation. But because she was human we know she had one. Part of the problem with some who are now walking in a greater degree of fullness is that we experience what we believe to be Naomi and Joseph like beauty in our living, but deny that we were ever ugly ducklings along the way. This book may appeal to only those of us who start out like Jacob. This book is for those of us who know what it is to lie, scheme, deceive and steal, but who are willing to go through the process of Christ being formed in us. This is for those of us who encounter the struggle it involves and the pain it sometimes brings and go on pursuing flight anyhow.

Truly, our struggle is not saving faith that leads to eternal life. We absolutely believe He's King of Kings and Lord of

Lords. Our struggle is finding the way to the high life ordained by that King and Lord during this temporary life span on earth.

Jacob is one of our leading men in this regard. It is Jacob who leads us to Jesus because Jacob knows sin and yet is striving to know God. If we were honest, we would say that this is where we are.

Frankly, the witness to a man (Jesus) who was fully human and yet knew no sin is foreign to me. Christ's most powerful appeal to me in this season of my life toward fullness is not that He knew no sin, but that through His death on the cross He has taken care of the sin I knew, do now know and tomorrow will know. That's ultimately the substance of my shout! It is Jacob, Rahab and David who most effectively show me that I too am a candidate for holiness and salvation. Joseph and Naomi testify to the fact that flying is possible. But Rahab and David show me what it takes to fly and that:

I too can make it from here. I too can fly.

You can make it from here. You can fly, no matter how far you've strayed or how long you've been cooped up. As long as you're on the right road, the skies of spiritual fullness belong to you. What is that road? The Point of No Return. Jacob knew this road in that he refused to let go of God. God had started something by apprehending him. Now, Jacob was going to make sure God finished it by not letting Him go. This is part of Jacob's contribution to the fullness.

Jacob's life proves that God can handle our flaws. What God finds hard to bless is the one who at any given moment is on the brink of returning to life without Him. Indeed, God does not ignore our character flaws. Certainly our journeys can be negatively influenced by our bad decisions or ethical set-backs. But our character flaws do not disqualify us from the spiritual high life. You still qualify! If Jacob does, so do you!

One night this scheming character named Jacob, harassed and distressed over past wrongs done by him and to him, was visited by God. God interrupted Jacob's sleep and started a tussle.

"Then Jacob was left alone; a Man wrestled with him until the breaking of day. Now when He saw that He did not prevail against him, He touched the socket of his hip; and the socket of Jacob's hip was out of joint as He wrestled with him. And He said, 'Let Me go, for the day breaks.' But he said, 'I will not let You go unless you Bless me.' "
— *Genesis 32:22-26*

Jacob is often labeled by many as a liar, schemer, deceiver and headstrong thief. But the flipside of Jacob is that he was on the right road. He refused to let go of God. A most important discipline in journey to flight is that discipline of persisting in God. Persistence leads us to a multitude of greatly sought-after secret desires, some of which we ourselves are not even aware of. But notice that we must be willing to persist, sometimes even amid the pain and wounds of the process.

THE WOUNDS THAT WIN
There are wounds that win. We know this. Isaiah tells us that, "He was wounded for our transgressions" *(Isaiah 53:1-3)*. Because of Christ's wounds we have victory over death. Jacob's life too shows forth the paradox of woundedness. His persistence through the night and his willingness to suffer the wound

in the night won him the desire of his heart. It was Jacob's refusal to let go, to turn back, which positioned him to receive the wound that won the victory.

The wounds that win are inflicted in hard struggle when God is changing our character and our natures. God refuses to bless us without changing us. Go through the night, you conqueror, so that God can work in the night releasing break-of-day blessing. Daytime glory is won in nighttime struggle during those hours when it's easier to let go of God. Eagles hold on until daybreak, even when it hurts. What was the result: Jacob proceeded limping but walking straight!

Jacob's wound is presented as a physical one apparently caused by the strike of the hand. But the real touch was deeper than his flesh. God disabled Jacob's hip. At the same time God enabled his spirit. And this had to be done if Jacob was going to receive the secret desires of his heart.

ALL YOU REALLY WANT

For a moment let's ask ourselves what Jacob really wants. On the surface the answer to this question is simple. He wants his brother's birthright and his father's blessing, correct? Obviously, this much is true. At Esau's point of desperation, Jacob manipulates a deal for his birthright. Later Jacob goes undercover to obtain his father's blessing, something that again belongs to someone else. Through these lenses we see a man bound by selfishness, chained by covetousness and willing to lie, deceive and steal to get what he wants. This accurate but surface view of Jacob is even reinforced within the birth narratives as we see him grabbing hold of his brother's foot in an apparent attempt to be the first born which carries along with it incomparable blessings from his father Isaac.

*"So when the days were fulfilled for her to give birth,
indeed there were twins in her womb. And the first
came out red. He was like a hairy garment all over; so they
called his name Esau. Afterward his brother
came out and his hand took hold of Esau's heel; so his
name was called Jacob..."*
— *Genesis 25:24-26*

I don't know about you, but I am first utterly baffled by this birth narrative. Then I am in total awe and intrigue at what such an act by Jacob in the birth canal means. There has got to be more to this man's story, and thus this man, than meets the eye. Whether you hold a literalist view of the scriptures or not, you still must be fascinated at this narrative.

If in your view this birth narrative is merely the creative genius of the faith community of that time trying to communicate a message about how it interprets the voice and acts of Yahweh, then you have to be impressed by the design of such a plot.

On the other hand, if such an act really did take place at the moment of birth, how does one account for the level of consciousness required within baby Jacob to reach out and attempt to "supplant" his twin brother Esau who somehow is emerging before him and instead of him from the womb?

Baffled, awed and intrigued, I have mostly questions and few if any answers about this narrative. Let me start with some questions that I think will intrigue you also. But be warned that these questions may serve to cast suspicion and doubt on the interpretive conclusions you may have drawn before about the entire Isaac household drama. I am not here to undergird previously held interpretations. I am here to ask new questions and prayerfully arrive at deeper truth and revelation for my flight.

In trying to understand this unthinkable, unheard of, unimaginable act of grabbing Esau's heel in the birth canal maybe it is necessary to ask what has never been thought, heard or imagined. I raise the following:

What transpired in the womb *before* the moment of birth, *before* it is revealed that in the birth canal Jacob reaches out to grab his brother's heel?
We see in the narrative *what Jacob does* in the birth canal which arouses our judgment of him,
but we do not have the benefit of seeing in the narrative what may have been done to Jacob which might enlighten our understanding of him.
Plainly put, is it possible that Jacob is not the supplanter, but in reality the supplanted?!!!

Could it be that he is the victim rather than the villain? Is it possible that Jacob is the one taken from as opposed to the taker? Could he be the one stolen from rather than the thief?

Yahweh is clear that within the womb of Rebekah there is a struggle between the two twins. Yahweh says to Rebekah, "The older (Esau) shall serve the younger (Jacob)." *(Genesis 25:22-24)* Note that it is Yahweh who announces this future state of affairs in the text. So we are made aware of the struggle between the two in the womb. But we are also made aware of a quirky, yet divinely authorized reversal within the pending future events because for the older to serve the younger is out of harmony with religious, social and cultural norms of that day.

Yahweh fully expects that Jacob will lose the battle in the womb but win the war in the end. Though he is last, he shall be first. He fully expects that Jacob's start has nothing to do with his finish, except that it will fuel a fire in him that will not be quenched until he has what he really wants: *The Full Blessing of a Son*!

Jacob was determined to be the head and not the tail, to receive the full and not the lesser of the inheritance of a son, wanting only the fullest a son could receive. And in his case, he wanted only what it appears from a larger view God ordained for him to have anyway.

What are we saying? Eagles only want what's coming to them; not from their fathers, mothers, churches, political parties or denominations, but from God Himself. They don't rest until they get it.

As leaders, whenever we hinder God's work in people by judging them, labeling them, closing doors on them or disqualifying them when we don't have a total picture of their journey, their time in the womb, we'd better make sure we ourselves are ready to be judged by those same measures. God will deal with us not based upon His tender mercies, but instead based upon how we have dealt with others. We'd better be trying to find ways to include people in what we call "our" ministries rather than authorizing ourselves as gate keepers and locking them out.

All Jacob really wants is what it appears he innately knew was coming to him even from the womb: the fullness of God's blessing. We should always remember that there are encounters, promises, visions, dreams, purposes within people that are hidden from our eyes just as what God planned for Jacob was hidden from his own father's and brother's eyes. Often the most important information about someone is what remains undisclosed. Never underestimate or fail to take into account what God has done or said that you are not privy to involving people. Birthing is public. But what happens in the womb is private. Our God of compassion transfers to us unspeakable desire for fullness in the hidden place of divine design.

For those of us who know what it means to be the Jacob of the house, take courage. There are going to be persons who disagree with your destiny, misunderstand your mission, challenge your choices and attack your tactics. Part of it will be because they weren't there in the womb, the private place, where the God of compassion told you that He has a place for you, too.

There are folks who will not understand your praise, your passion, your conviction or your strivings simply because they weren't in the womb with you. It was in the womb that God designed, out of His compassion, your flight plans. Don't get angry or upset or frustrated or disappointed with them, they just weren't there!

Jacob's act of grabbing the heel of Esau was an act of desperation born out of the pending danger to his future destiny of being fully blessed. The fight for your destiny is the fight for your life that never should have been threatened anyway. And that's the lesson we've missed. The indictment should not be put upon Jacob nor Esau, but rather upon any familial, social,

THE WAY OF AN EAGLE

religious, economic or cultural system that leaves people behind, in danger and at risk. The new revelation is that there don't have to be winners and losers. God urges all of us through Jacob to hear what He has reserved for even those who are the left behind and the locked out. Some of us have been searching high and low, devising and plotting, in efforts to receive that which seems missing from our lives. This just in from heaven: **All you really want is the fullness of God's blessing!**

> *"And He said, 'Your name shall no longer*
> *be called Jacob, but Israel;*
> *for you have struggled with God and with men,*
> *and have prevailed.'*
> *… And He blessed him here."*
> — ***Genesis 32:28-29***

Alas! What Jacob desired all along — Heaven's Blessing! From here everything changes. Jacob arises from his struggle with God proving that he is in it to win it. Limping but walking straight, the man arose with the sun upon him, the old nature behind him, a nation's sons around him and victory before him — all because he persisted in struggle and would not turn away from God's deep dealings in the night. From here Jacob must do no more tricking, scheming, lying or deceiving. In fact he never had to. All that he wanted was supposed to be his anyway. The best way to ensure that what is transferred in the womb manifest after birth is to strive with God and not let go.

YOU ARE ACQUITTED
There are multitudes of men and women within the

Kingdom of God who possess within them secret desires of experiencing the fullness of the blessing of God in every area of their lives. The spiritual, financial, emotional, social and mental fullness we secretly desire is legitimate. We often grope and groan for fullness in marriage, ministry, community and so on, not recognizing that these desires are both authentic and authorized. We are freed to take Godly pursuit of these desires when we begin to make them known and watch every perceived limitation or obstacle bow.

We are often made to feel guilty or bad about wanting the fullness of God. Likewise, measures we are sometimes led to take in order to arrive at fullness can result in criticism and disapproval. Many of us can say that we took questionable courses to obtain sound ends. Our motives may have been good, but our strategies needed refining. For all of those whose motives have been pure, Christ proclaims, "Blessed are the pure in heart for they shall see God" *(Matthew 5:8)*. God measures us by the conditions of our hearts. David's value to God and favor before God as a man after God's own heart was illustrated by God's ability to see through his tactics to his heart. David's acts were no more or less treacherous than anyone before him or since him. The difference has to be none other than God's ability to see something in people that we can't. If you're reading this and you are still yoked by the guilt of bad stuff you did out of good intentions, then today is your day of release. You are acquitted. Do not let enter into your life another person or thought which functions to grip you in the shame of past actions taken with good intentions at heart. Don't worry, somebody somewhere knows your heart and what God has planned for you.

Every now and then God will send somebody your way who knows what you know about God's plan for you and affirm the legitimacy and authority of the secret desires that reside within you. As one who is anointed to found churches and birth ministers, I know well the struggles associated with the process of being designed in God's womb and striving toward fullness amid criticism. In my deepest hours of despair and anxiety, God has sent unlikely and unexpected people to remind me that the work is not in vain and that this mission is His.

Because of where I've arisen from, I have difficulty accepting that I too can receive the promises of God. In my environment much was taken from me, and I witnessed a great deal pass me by. The notion of having anything bestowed upon me was an idea I had to get used to. Recently, I was picked up by surprise at my home one Sunday morning and taken for a drive by a Mexican brother named Jesus Rodriguez. Jesus, nicknamed "Chewey," joined Mountaintop our first year in operation and was baptized along with his children. He picked me up at our home and took me for an hour-long drive and poured into me all God was trying to say that I could not hear because of where I had come from. His words were not eloquent or sophisticated, but filled with power:

"Pastor, you're doing it. You're preaching God's word. People are being saved. People are being touched. You have a nice family and a nice home. You deserve it, Pastor. You deserve everything you got."

These were simple yet powerful words for me. I had let slip from my mind the heavenly value of the seventy souls baptized, the twelve ministers licensed, the six elders ordained, the four couples led into Christian marriage, and the host of individuals blessed by the ministry in five years since it emerged from the womb. His loving heart and broken English spoke to my spirit which was burdened by regrets involving the past and doubts regarding the future. Chewey knew what God had for me. Believe this, somebody knows what God has for you. And even if they don't know what it is, they know it's something great. Sometimes that's all you need to help take you to the next level.

All charges have been dropped and you're on the right road. Don't you dare think about turning back now!

CHAPTER V

Missing Your Plane and Catching Your Flight

ALL ABOARD!

Now you know for sure that you're not crazy. All of the tossing and turning was because you were haunted by the Holy. God is moving you out of mediocrity. You've faced your burden to soar. You're dealing with what you want.

You've relocated yourself now; not necessarily to a new city, but to a new source of power. You've got the Hook-Up. It's not a new hairstyle, wardrobe, job, house or dose of viagra. It's not a new drug, new stimulant or a new mate. It's not even a new attitude, because that will not even suffice with where you're going. You have arrived at a position to receive new spiritual strength. And it may be that nothing has really changed around you … not yet anyway. It is how you see God that has changed. Thus, how you see yourself, your obstacles, your setbacks and your opportunities has changed as well. You know now that you were made to fly.

You've identified your coops. You've called by name those people, places and things that no longer or never did serve in your launch. You've exposed those elements in your life which hem you in and dry you out. You're cooped up, but that's all right because you will not be there long. Your divorce papers have been sent. You're ready to fly.

You're even on the right road now. You've reached the critical point in your journey that guarantees success — The Point of No Return. You've released everybody who has habitually labeled, judged, criticized or excluded you simply because they fail to understand you and what God designed for you in the womb even before you appeared. Ain't no turning back now!

But as we mount up like wings of an eagle as God has promised, how will we know when we're flying and who shall lead the way? The answer to both of these questions is Jesus the Christ. He is the model of spiritual flight for the Believer. His life and ministry, more than anyone else, provide for us revelation into what it means to fly. Let us look no further than the Author and Finisher of our faith.

My closer look at Jesus as a model for my flight began on the July 26, 2000. On this day God apprehended me privately while in prayer and impressed upon my spirit that He was about to take me to a new level that I hadn't yet experienced. This is why a time of listening to and for God is critical in our intimacy with Him. Often He wants to talk also.

My closer look at Jesus gained more depth on April 8, 2001. Increasingly, the ministry God led me to plant had begun to plateau in terms of numbers. Our steady growth in membership from the founding 15 members to 105 in the first two years was a cause for celebration and hope. But in 2000 that trend changed. Our membership began to decrease. Some leaders began to doubt and rebel. Our numbers got to as low as fifty. Encouraged by a member, I visited a church in Bakersfield, CA, on April 7 to share the vision for our ministry in hopes that they would sow into Mountaintop financially. But it was the following day, April 8, when the breakthrough occurred.

That Sunday morning I visited the Koinonia Full Gospel

Christian Church in Los Angeles for worship before my return to Tucson. It was Palm Sunday. Bishop Gregory Davis from Louisiana was visiting on this Sunday. The pastor of Koinonia had recently died and Bishop Davis was being considered for the pastorate. I found an immediate spiritual connection with this man and knew immediately that God had ordained my presence at Koinonia that morning. As I knew would happen, I received the "Word of the Lord." What I didn't know is that God would speak prophetically through Bishop Davis directly to me. I shall never forget this day, for it helped to chart my course for flight and flame the fire for this book. Bishop Davis had never met me. He had no prior knowledge of my position or service in the Kingdom of God. For all he knew I was just another member there at Koinania. Flowing prophetically, he turned to me and asked me to stand. He asked me where I was from and if I was a pastor. Overflowing in the love and power that is only of God he opened his mouth. God told me five things through Bishop Davis on that day. They were:

1. **He was going to meet every budgetary need.**
2. **There was going to be an increase of the anointing over my life and ministry.**
3. **I was going to receive a refreshing from the Lord.**
4. **Challengers to the ministry at home were going to bow.**
5. **God was going to turn my tears to joy.**

Always remember that even when you don't get the job, if you obey the Lord, you can still get the job done. Bishop Davis did not return to pastor Koinania. But I returned to Tucson to pastor Mountaintop with a refreshing from God that I cannot put into words. Bishop Davis didn't get the job, but he did the job. The following day at LAX I sat awaiting my plane in deep meditation and prayer. I turned to my journal and began to write what is here in the next chapter called the seven dimensions of the anointing of the Holy Ghost, or the seven dimensions of flight.

When I returned to consciousness an hour later and went to the ticket counter with my little orange rectangular boarding pass that only Southwest passengers can appreciate, the lady said to me:

"Are you Mr. Howard?"
I replied, "Yes, I am."
She said, "Sir, your plane left forty five minutes ago.
We called your name over and over again,
but you did not respond. I'm sorry,
but we'll have to book you on the next plane out."

I may have missed my plane, but I caught my flight. There are many lessons here. Beloved foremost is, never doubt what God can do even if you have to take a later flight. Never let regrets of the past hinder you from taking the next flight available toward spiritual excellence. Other opportunities have passed, but the one before you is available. Oh, hear this today. Every moment in the Kingdom of God there is a flight taking off toward grace, forgiveness, restoration, renewal, hope and power. Even if you missed the last one, let this one be yours. Can't you hear Jesus, the flight commander, calling you?

Well, the church at Bakersfield never gave a penny. But the trip wasn't about finding money. It was about finding higher dimensions in Christ. The leaders whose motives were bad began to bow and go to other ministries. I came home with renewed power to finish the work of establishing Mountaintop. I started this book you're reading right now. I rebuked demons which tried to break my spirit. I am overcoming my own weaknesses and frailties. I confronted my own hurts and wounds, allowing the anointing to heal me. Now, there is no more weeping. Only tears of joy.

AN ALTERED STATE

In a closer look at Jesus the Christ, our model for flight, it is clear that at least three factors conjoined to comprise such powerful works of ministry. One was the essential substance of His being — He was the Original Seed of immortality for the redemption of humanity. Thus He is called in Corinthians the "firstfruits" of those of us who will take on the full essence of what it means to be immortal. His essential substance was fully God, thus He displayed all of the characteristics of immortality that we too are now, and will completely, display also *(1Corinthians 15:21-23).* This is what it means to have it said that "we shall be like Him" *(I John 3:1-2).* His culminating act displaying the essential substance of immortality occurred in the Resurrection where He dealt the final blow to death, thereby countering mortality's most profound nemesis.

A second factor that helped to make possible such acts of power in ministry was His disposition of submission. Though He was fully divine, we know also that He was fully human, like us in ways which included capacities for sin and evil. Thus it is said that He too "was tempted in all ways" such as we are. Yet, He yielded not *(Hebrews 4:15).* This refusal to yield to sin and evil was eclipsed and dependent, however, upon His disposition of total submission to God. *(Philippians 2:7-8)*. In Him there was total submission to the Father; thus there was fullness of power.

A third factor stems from His spiritual condition or "state" which in turn explains the identification of Him as the "Messiah" (Hebrew/Old Testament) or "Christ" (Greek/New Testament). These respective names speak to both His identity as the "One" who is to redeem, and likewise, the "One" who possesses special capability to do such. This is illustrated in the question of John the Baptist in his own hour of ultimate sacrifice. The forerunner calls for an inquiry of the "One" who it appears he anticipated would be the emerging hope for salvation. The stakes were so high, the need so great and the longings so deep that John the Baptist asked for the inquiry to be stated in a two-fold form: "Are you the Coming One, or do we look for another *(Luke 7:18-19)*? On the table are two critical issues of our faith. Jesus, are you willing? Jesus, are you able?

This combination of being uniquely chosen (appointed) and capable (anointed) to redeem rendered Him as not only Jesus, but also Christ. In this He announces Himself to be under a peculiar state:

> *"The Spirit of the Lord is upon Me,*
> *because He has anointed me..."*
> *— Luke 4:18*

We see through the scriptures in the life, preaching and outreach of this Christ seven dimensions of this peculiar state Mary's firstborn says He is under. This anointing, this altered state, can be defined as the divine energy and divine effects of the Spirit of God. It was under this anointing, this peculiar condition we term an altered state, that He flowed. He was both energized and effective in living a life of fullness in this altered state. It was as Jesus he came out from Mary, a Palestinian Jew in an impoverished Nazarene community. It was as Christ He came out from God under the anointing of the Holy Ghost in an altered state in order to preach, redeem, heal and deliver.

Our blessing on the way to flight is that we too have an anointing of that same Spirit. We too can enter into that which we term an altered state in order to alter the seemingly unalterable conditions of our mortal existence. This is part of the Good News — that Jesus saves and gives unto us the power, the anointing, to live out that salvation within the existential realities of the world around us. This is not a call to take on some alien personality and character. We are not here involved in the theatrics of fictional musing or role-playing. This is a call to enter into that realm of spirituality Jesus dwelt within, completely submerged in the influence and power of the divine. As He is the "Christos" (Grk) or Anointed One, we are the Christians, Anointed Ones who progressively share in the same benefits as He while living under this peculiar state.

There exists a unity in and with Him that is proclaimed by Him. He tells His disciples that He is in the Father, the Father is in Him and that they (we) are in Him (Jesus) *(John 14:20)*. This perfect unity is activated by the coming of the Helper, the Anointer, the Holy Spirit. Because Jesus dwelt in high places in the Father, we can dwell in high places for we are in Him and He is in us.

As we take another look at the Christ, it is possible to identify Seven Dimensions He flourished in as He lived, preached, taught and ministered under the altered state of the anointing.

We know that we are soaring when we witness our own advance, brought about by the anointing, in the following areas that issue forth next.

CHAPTER VI

The Seven Dimensions of the Anointing

AND YOU SHALL KNOW THE TRUTH…

The foundation dimension of the anointing stirring our initial flight is the Spirit's revelation of truth. By the anointing of the Holy Spirit we are enabled to believe, understand and know truth so that we are dependent not upon the wisdom of men or the intellectual disciplines formed by mortal ingenuity. *(I John 2:20,26,27; I Corinthians 2:9-12).*

All academic disciplines such as philosophy, science, mathematics and so on are human attempts to explain or arrive at truth, or that which is supreme reality, that which ultimately exists. Christ was under such an anointing that He not only confessed to lead others to the ultimate reality who is God; He declared in full confidence of the truth concerning Himself, "I am the way, the truth and the life" *(John 14:6)*.

He is the Anointed One who, by paradox, is and leads us into the ultimate and supreme reality who is God. The religion of the Pharisees and other sects of the Jewish elite in the first century did not satisfy, in Christ's estimation, the demands of "bearing witness" to that truth who is God *(John 18:37)*. Theirs, it appears from Jesus' words, was the sin of not being true to God, or not adequately reflecting His glory.

Thus, it is said by Christ regarding His disciples that we "shall know the truth …" through the anointing of the "Spirit of Truth" which moves in concert with His word *(John 8:31)*. The promise is that we shall know the truth, meaning we will possess cognitive understanding and, unlike the first century religious elite, adequately reflect the truth in our deeds as well. This is how it shall make us free. All Kingdom affairs start, stay and end here at this dimension of the revelation of truth so as to counter the continual lies the enemy advances in an effort to misrepresent the Father and subvert or redirect the glory that belongs to God.

Now, there are multitudes of persons who come to know, believe or understand basic truth about the existence and reality of God through means of reason or the "wisdom of the world." But these individuals lack the anointing to respond with their lives in such a way that they bear full witness of God through Christ, which is the only adequate response *(I Corinthians 1:20)*.

The anointing of the Holy Spirit causes a response from the anointed ones in a depth and manner that truth demands and deserves. The only appropriate response to the truth who is God, is the laying down of one's life. The Anointed One set the model on the cross and calls upon us to pick up ours as well. Then He gives His anointing to activate us. Knowing the truth is giving your life to the Christ who is truth. Anything short of this uncovers a breach in the believer's spirituality and a need for prayer that a greater anointing would be released within. Christ's confidence in this work within us is great. This is evidenced in His prophetic statement: **"... and the truth shall make you free"** *(John 8:32)*.

Finally, Christ's greatest challenge with regard to these matters was to endure in the belief of the truth regarding Himself. Amid all the perverted reports about Him, He kept His feet to the path the Father had ordered. He kept His ears to the message his Father had sent. He was the Son of God. His holding to this truth made Him steadfast in His mission to die and rise again. Had He not believed this truth, we would have to look in futility for another. Thank you, Jesus, for being and believing truth. Release now in greater measure the anointing we already have that we may soar with You!

YOUR NAME IS WRITTEN … NOW STIR IT UP!

Christ responded to the truth about Himself in many ways. The most noteworthy relative to our salvation was His response in dying and raising again. He did this, according to our faith, in His own self realization as the Lamb of God who was to counter the sin predicament of humanity.

A second dimension of His anointing is indicated by His inaugural message noted earlier from Luke 4. Like most initial messages, or first sermons, He states what God has done, is doing and will do. But unlike most coming-out messages, He announces that all God is doing is being fulfilled in Him! What a radical notion! Think about it. His announcement is the first of many to indicate that He Himself is the one, true and only Savior of the world. The second dimension of the anointing has to do with the practices of ministry performed on the mission; the particular acts taken to fulfill it. Christ was anointed to do!

You are not just anointed to believe, understand and know truth. You are anointed to respond to that truth in significant ways to advance the Kingdom of God. The anointing **activates the believer** in this second dimension. It gives the energy and effectiveness in ministry practices and the stirring of gifts. It activates us to do.

And hear this well, only the anointing activates. This is part of why Jesus never sought authority or freedom from anybody to do anything. Even as a youngster of twelve or so, the anointing was beginning to stir Him. In response, He hangs back with the religious elites in Jerusalem whom He witnesses doing what He sees Himself evolving to do also — submit to religious practices and leadership. When Mary asks Him in scolding tone where He'd been, He returned her scorn as if to imply she should have known that He had to be about His Father's business *(Luke 2:49-50)*. Well, Joseph's business was done in Jerusalem so He couldn't have been speaking of him. Hence, His transformation from Mary's Baby to God's Son was now in full swing. He sought, quite naturally without consideration it seems, no permission to hang back with the big fellows to observe and participate in the discussions of His Father's work and will. He couldn't help Himself. He was responding to the unfolding activation. Really, what He is announcing in Luke 4, two chapters and eighteen years later, is that He's been activated by the anointing. Indeed, those under the anointing are gripped by an unexplainable authority and focus such as was Jesus at twelve years old. This does not excuse us from healthy covenants with Spirit-filled people and networks to hold us accountable. But it does highlight a truth that cannot go in error – men do not activate or de-activate you. God does.

Every eagle has an activation testimony, a story about the realization of an unyielding power inside of you to do. For those who are called to ministry as a profession often a starting place is seminary. Mine was Central Baptist Theological Seminary in Kansas City, Kansas. My journey there was filled with wonder and challenges as I was preparing to be released into a life of full-time ministry. One of the events that transformed me most was my encounter with the president of the seminary at that time, Dr. Thomas Clifton. It was my final year in seminary, and like all seniors I had the responsibility of leading and preaching at the seminary community's weekly worship services on campus. The focus of my message was Jesus' call of Lazarus from the grave. My thesis centered upon the human act involved in the divine miracle when those who were present at the point of need received the command of Jesus to "take away the stone" (John 11:38). I pointed out that all of us have had people in our lives whose shoulders we stand upon, people who played a vital role in moving stones and allowing us to arrive at the point of responding to the call of ministry upon our lives.

To bring the thesis into context, I noted that seminaries are supposed to be places where ministers and lay people experience stones being taken away so that they can be released to perform the ministry tasks we've already been activated by the anointing to engage. This central theme was accentuated by the imagery of Christ in the Garden of Gethsemane praying for strength. Luke records that in Jesus' hour of greatest soul searching He adjusted His location to an area that was a "stone's throw away" (a small distance) in the process of arriving at that place of harmony with the will of God for His life. Undoubtedly, the stone moved from the tomb of Lazarus was moved not very far, but just far enough to no longer be an impediment to his breakout. Sometimes a small distance can make such a huge difference in someone's breakthrough. We don't always have to do earth-shattering things to participate in the miracle of God in people's lives. Just move a stone! The Divine will cause the quake! Sometimes God reserves the working of the miracle for Himself.

As president of the student association of the seminary my senior year, I had experienced pleasant exchanges with Dr.

Clifton before. But on this day after I preached, he pulled me aside and began to pour affirmations of truth within me and spoke prophetically about my future, impacting me in ways that to this day he probably does not realize. He did not authorize me, nor did he seek to. But he did affirm me. He acclaimed me, but he did not activate me. Authentic effective leaders like Tom Clifton know how to move stones, in this case speak life, as the human involvement in the appearance of the miracles of God *(Proverbs 10:11)*. I left seminary nurtured and confident in the God who called me. Yet I was challenged enough to still understand how small and needy I was. Starting a car is one thing, shifting to drive and moving into heavy traffic is another. If God said through Dr. Clifton and the seminary, "Be released," when or how had He already said "come alive" or start your engine?

My activation took place about nine months before I entered seminary. Struggling with and resisting God's call to preach, I had fled from worship one Sunday morning with tears in my eyes. I sensed God was calling me to preach, but I had fears and doubts within me. On this day in October of 1990, I was filled with the Spirit while praising God in worship at the St. Stephen Baptist Church in Kansas City, Missouri, my church home where Dr. Mac Charles Jones, pastor and prophet, was my pastor and mentor. I ran out of the choir stand and out of the church in the middle of the song we were singing. I then got into my car and drove over to Linwood and Benton Boulevards, the streets on which I spent much of my time playing as a little kid. I got out of my car and began to walk west on Linwood Boulevard toward Prospect Ave., taking the same route I would take some seventeen years earlier when Grandma Rowena would send me up to the Rexall store to get medicine for her arthritis or bread or milk. At this moment never had I felt so apprehended, so taken over, so frustrated with putting something off. As I walked, I cried profusely, scared to believe, yet in awe of this Otherness that continued to pursue me as I came to the realization reluctantly that this appeared to really be God calling me?!!! Before in my refusal to surrender to the call, the only remaining excuse had been that the relentless burden I was experiencing relative to becoming a minister was just the lure of the illusions of power, control, fame and the so-called good life. But because of my depth of relationship with Dr. Jones, I was exposed to the personal costs and depth of sacrifice necessary to really honor God in the ministry. "Mac" was, without doubt, one of the most prophetic voices and activists for peace, justice and human rights in Kansas City and across the country and world. The dynamism of his anointing sent him to boldly challenge public policy in Washington, D.C., and yet sent him also to draw gang members in reconciliation and peace. His effectiveness, however, had costs. He was highly misunderstood by many in the local body who were not ready or just disagreed with the bold ways God would use him. He was before his time as he brought a new paradigm of ministry that embraced women as preachers, welcomed the outcasts into the center of the life of the church and established outreach ministries that sought to build economic development in the community. A lot of what is considered cutting edge today was presented by him in the late '80s and early '90s. I was close enough to see the attacks upon him, and most of them came from within the church rather than outside of it. Much like Jesus, Mac was greatly honored and sought after away from home and abroad, but sadly misunderstood and sorely under-appreciated by many at home. Thus, I was not delusional about ministry. I had eyes wide open. I had become privy to the private pains, sufferings, attacks and challenges of ministers.

I stopped walking short of Prospect Ave. on the corner of Montgall Ave and Linwood and raised my voice to heaven, saying to God that if this was Him He was going to have to make it crystal clear or else I wasn't doing anything or going anywhere. At that moment I looked down at the sidewalk I was standing on and written into the cement was my name as if it had been etched in the concrete ...V E R N O N. I stood there standing, floored. A month later I quit my job. Three months after that I was licensed to preach by Dr. Jones and St. Stephen. Six months after that I entered seminary. Three years after that I took on the pastorate of my first church. Three years after that I raised up a new church. In the middle I earned a doctorate. By the grace of God over two-hundred have been baptized, thousands have heard the gospel. My mistakes have been many. But through it all God's anointing has empowered since the first day it activated me. Whenever trials threaten to clip my wings, I pull out a picture I later took of that sidewalk to remind me who sent me. Your name, too, has been etched in the purposes of God. You too have an anointing. When you get your release ... Stirrrrrrr it up!!!

RADICAL RESISTANCE AND OPPOSITION TO SIN AND EVIL

As we delve deeper, a third dimension of the anointing is revealed after the baptism of Christ, yet before He is released to set His ministry in motion. Once He is grounded in truth and activated by the anointing, He is not led directly to the crowds to hold massive healing services, build mega churches or draw thousands by virtue of His capabilities. No! First, He is led by the same Spirit He declared anointed Him into the wilderness to be tempted by the devil. Herein is revelation of the third dimension of the anointing *(Matthew 4:1-11)*.

Before Christ's ministry unfolds outwardly, something had to be settled inwardly. The issue that had to be resolved, could only be put to rest in conflict with the powers of darkness. The issue was: where He stood regarding sin and evil?.

The lesson is that the anointing develops within us a radical resistance and opposition to sin and evil. In the final analysis the gifts we stir in ministry are aimed at freeing people from the powers of sin and evil which grip them. God will not have us to be activated and released into ministry with knowledge of truth, yet unarmed with a deep sense of His vengeance which drives the righteous reversal He promises will spring forth from those under the anointing *(Isaiah 61:2)*. We must be clear and present danger to the powers of darkness in our private personal lives as we are released to challenge them in public. Biblical examples are present involving folks who ventured out to confront a particular nature of adversarial power in public without having settled their victory over those same satanic powers in private *(Mark 9:14-29; Acts 19:13-15)*.

This dimension of the anointing is in harmony with the Spirit's overall and general work of restraining evil in the world *(2 Thessalonians 2:7)*. This restraining work is made contextual and particular as He operates within the giftings, callings and offices of the church.

Demonstrated in this dimension of the anointing is our understanding of who the enemy is *(Ephesians 5:12)*. Brought to light is both a disposition of opposition against the adversary and a gained position of private victory over the adversary. In this dimension we are energized and developed increasingly both against and over spiritual wickedness. This disposition against and positioning over was won by Christ and passed on to us in His death, burial and resurrection *(Ephesians 4:9-12)*. It is our task in flight to take it upon us and live it out under the anointing.

PROGRESSIVE AND PIONEERING OBEDIENCE

Central to all the dimensions of the anointing is the work done in progressing us in obedience, for this is the highest sacrifice one can make to God. In other places this work of the Spirit is called sanctification — to make or to be holy. Progressive and pioneering obedience is what we actually experience during that process of living out that state of holiness the Bible calls sanctification.

It is necessary to draw distinctions and point out the parallels of these associated phenomena because sanctification/holiness is such a broader work than obedience and is accomplished in two ways. Firstly, we have become sanctified or holy by virtue of the blood of Christ which is a status made available to us *(1 Peter 1:2)*.

Secondly, in response to that status, we are to live a sanctified or holy life in deed and conduct which is won by measurable behavior to moral standards *(Leviticus 19:1-2; Ephesians 1:4)*. The first, then, is a status granted by accepting the cleansing work of Christ. The other is a status gained by your own holy works. It is progressive and pioneering obedience that is furthered in the second regard of advancing in holy practices. Obedience involves human action and decision in living out moral imperatives. These acts and decisions are empowered by the energy of the Holy Spirit. Believers trust in this power to energize us to obedience. New attitudes or natural motivations toward these ends may cease or wane. The anointing is a constant power available at all times.

This link between the anointing and obedience is key. We are perplexed and discouraged, even driven away from the church, in the face of those who experience moral failure and setbacks shouting, "Those hypocrites, those hypocrites!" We fail to understand that just as all believers need room to grow in the release of the anointing in their practice of gifts, they also need room to grow in the release of the anointing in greater obedience. The same Spirit who anoints us to stir the gift to teach or preach is the same Spirit who anoints us to obey ethical commands — it's just another dimension! Hypocrisy is not failure to be perfect. It is pretending to be perfect when you are not.

We pray for a greater release of the anointing to obey the Lord in order to show forth His ever increasing glory on earth *(2 Cor. 3:18)*. This is why the anointing works to make us more and more obedient over time (progressive) and obedient in new areas (pioneering) — it is to honor the call unto us to move from glory, to glory, to glory!

DEEPENING LOVE AND DESIRE FOR GOD

A few years ago I was presented a certificate by the American Baptist Churches of the Pacific Southwest. The certificate was presented at a special equipping and fellowship gathering in Covina, CA. I was awarded with the "Inspire the Desire" award. Each church planter was given an award that best characterized the work they've done in planting churches in their cities. I never asked why I was given that particular award. The regional and state ministers who awarded it had participated with us in various ministry activities including the ordination of elders and the hosting of ABC National Ministries president Aidsand Wright Riggins, III, in celebration of our third year having birthed Mountaintop. I believe they gave this particular award because they saw something in our people at our gatherings — Desire! Many do not equate desire — deep depths of want or will — with the anointing. Scripture reveals we could and probably should.

The Bible is clear that the Holy Spirit, as a personality, possesses a will or desire. Jesus declares "the Spirit is willing but the flesh is weak" *(Matthew 26:41)*. It is possible then to speak of the "will of the Spirit" or to make a determination of what the Spirit's desires are.

In the Johannine gospel Jesus reveals the ultimate will or desire of the Spirit is the glorification of the Father — or the full recognition, acknowledgment, praise and honor of God *(John 16:14-15)*. His cause is God's glorification through the Son.

A question which follows: if the Holy Spirit, the anointer, possesses will or desires for the glorification of the Father, how deeply does the Spirit long for such? How bad does He want it? A clue to how bad He wants it is to survey how He "feels" when it doesn't occur or is denied. We know from scripture that it is possible for the Holy Spirit to be grieved *(Ephesians 4:30; Isaiah 63:10)*. Grieving is evidence of depth of desire and an orientation toward passion. We can conclude that the Holy Spirit desires or deeply wants with passion or great expression, the glorification and the will of God to take place. He wants it bad.

Dwelling within us, His anointing creates a heart condition consistent with the Holy Spirit's own desires and depth of expression. All of this streams from a mighty love that is shed abroad in our hearts by Him *(Romans 5:5)*.

This dimension of the anointing furthers the measure of our love for God. It is only by loving God deeper that we come to complete surrender to His will. There exists no other substitute than a heart after the presence, will and glory of God. It is this dimension of the anointing that sends us to the water brooks of God in prayer, fasting, praise, worship and study *(Psalm 42:1-2)*.

Deep love and passion for God can be measured by our worship in obedient deed, passionate response and emotional commitment. It flourishes in a love relationship with the Father nurtured by the anointing which makes God increasingly more our treasure *(Matthew 6:21)*.

HEALING OF THE HEART

Recently God broadened the scope of my ministry to reach into the academic arena. I believe that He is preparing me for service in seminary down the road. Currently I am teaching at the University of Arizona in African American religion and culture. One of my students this summer was NBA star Damon Stoudamire of the Portland Trailblazers. While Damon was taking my course, he made national headlines, but it wasn't because of his performance on the court. The week before he was to complete the course work, he was arrested for alleged marijuana possession. As I saw him file into court on the local news, my heart grieved for him because it had become clear that he was a good brother with a good heart and a bright mind. Immediately upon hearing the news, I sensed that his presence in my class was no accident.

This was confirmed for me the next day when he called and

began to fill me in on the details of his ordeal and assure me that he would fulfill all of his class attendance and work requirements. True to his word, he completed all course work, and his material was consistently excellent throughout the summer. But something more happened that week that the columnists and reporters who labeled and wrote him off do not know. After class on the last day of the summer session he gave his life to Christ.

During our time of talking, sharing and crying together, Damon discussed some off-the-court battles he had been facing and disclosed that even before the arrest God had been tugging on him. "Even before all this went down, V.P.," he said to me, "the Lord had been working on me." The tears that flowed from both of our eyes as we affirmed our respective hurts, weaknesses and setbacks resulted in a waterfall of joy as Damon surrendered to God's love. We prayed the prayer of faith as this under-sized young man who had always felt the burden to fight all of life's battles on his own came up big. We declared together and affirmed that it would be God who we would trust to fight our battles for us.

Later Damon shared that he opened up with me because he felt I was someone who would understand and not judge him, someone with whom he could let his guard down. I believe it is also because he and I share some of the same journey.

I shared with him how my lack of a father and an impoverished start caused me to resolve that if I were going to be successful I'd have to do it all myself. I knew that I would have to fight hard for everything that came my way because I had less to work with than others. This kind of "me against the world" mentality is developed when a young man refuses to give up on his dreams even though he lacks the resources around him to make that dream a reality. It is a weapon we use to rise above disadvantages we were born into and had nothing to do with. We become our own equalizers. We resolve to win at all costs, even if it means developing a gladiator-like outlook that drives us toward success. I am a witness that the load of carrying such weight gets too heavy to bear over time. The God-designed need for love, help and sharing in life soon catches up. The costs of such a mentality are detrimental. We modify our hearts. We turn them on and turn them off only when we want to; and never is our heart totally free.

But we were not intended to live under the illusion, or even live, period, without a communal village of aid and nurture to cradle our journeys. The God-designed need for love, help and sharing is demonstrated in the indigenous African philosophical view: "I am because we are." Our individuality grows out of the existence of the community. Therefore, the value of community and sharing in a context of love is supreme. Sooner or later, if we are blessed, the modified heart breaks down or melts under the pressure of God's love. That's what happened to me back in 1985 when I accepted Christ. I believe that's what happened to Damon on that day he said yes to the love of God.

What I had been teaching and preaching about the anointing was confirmed again on this day through Damon. He is a man with a good heart but was in need, like every other man alive, of the healing touch of God. Often are hearts are not bad, just bruised. Often they are not wicked, just wounded. One of the differences between Damon and the rest of us is that his frailty was public, while some of us have become sophisticated enough to keep ours private. In spite of news reports and predictions

**of his downfall, Damon is a winner who has arisen to
receive the anointing of the Holy Spirit to heal his heart.**

Christ spoke specifically to the power of the anointing to
heal the broken hearted and to give unto those who mourn in
Zion restoration, joy, hope and a reason for praise *(Isaiah 61:3)*.
There is no suitable or more effective ingredient to heal the
hearts of individuals. This healing ministry was a vital part of
the core of the ministry of Christ on earth. It remains a vital
part of the core of ours.

This dimension of the anointing, though readily available,
is not as easily attained or received. This is true because there
are so many proposed substitutes such as riches, human intimacy, substances such as marijuana or alcohol and a host of
other worldly pleasures.

Nevertheless, there is healing power if we allow ourselves
close enough to God to receive it. God promises healing to
those in Zion which in this dispensation is not a geographical
local on the map, but instead a spiritual local accessible to all in
the touch of His love and mercy. Praise God for Damon's
restoration and hope. Praise God for His anointing which heals
us to fulfill the moral, ethical and spiritual high call we all
would miss if it were not for the grace of God.

YOKES AND BONDAGES BROKEN IN AND AROUND YOU

In my ten years of pastoring God has graced me to midwife
the birth of ten ministers. Two currently are pending licensing
in respective stages of preparation. Part of that preparation
involves a focus on the ministers' spiritual formation. The individual is asked to prayerfully reflect and then write a document
detailing various aspects of their spiritual formation including:

personal mission statement, personal vision statement, testimony of conversion experience, testimony of their response to the call of ministry, identification of spiritual gifts, and last but not least — identification of yokes or bondages within them.

A yoke or bondage is a spiritual state of enslavement to anything that is unauthorized by the will of God *(Romans 8:14-15)*. Either our selfish indulgence or our failure to activate the power within us to overcome the yoke is at issue *(Romans 8:5; 1 John 4:4)*. In either case it is sin because it renders us subject to some other ruler *(Matthew 6:24)*.

Behind or in the yoke, demonic forces work to subvert the glory of God, shame the Kingdom of God, hinder the personal spiritual growth of the people of God, rob from the strength of the church of God, destroy the ministries of God and control families, communities and nations *(Ephesians 6:12)*.

Recall that it is in the third dimension of the anointing that a radical opposition and resistance to sin (yokes/bondages) is birthed and begins to develop. Here in the power of this seventh dimension these yokes are broken.

A number of scriptures speak to the power of the anointing of the Holy Spirit, or the anointing upon a servant stirred in action, to break or destroy yokes of all kind such as emotional, psychological, physical, political or religious *(2 Cor. 1:21; 1 John 2:20,27; 2 Cor. 3:17; Luke 4:18-19; Isaiah 61:1-3; Isaiah 59:19; Isaiah 9:4)*. It should be noted that yokes also manifest within the physical realm through political oppression, systems of economic exploitation, systemic poverty, violence and militarism, vain materialism, excessive consumerism, racism and sexism. Satanic powers either design or enter into these more systemic manifestations of yokes and bring about demonic ends *(John 10:10)*. All human affairs, whether in or out of the church, which result in ends that steal, destroy and deceive have the devil in the details somewhere some way. Our training as ministers involves a focus on yokes because we are to lead the body of Christ in teaching and living out the power of the anointing as we witness.

Christ's entire ministry on earth was the demonstration of the power of the anointing that rendered the yokes of satanic design fruitless in His being and in His life. He announced and warned beforehand of this:

"And now I have told you before it comes, that when it does come to pass you may believe ... for the ruler of this world is coming, he has nothing in Me."
— John 14:29-30

Herein the fullness of the anointing is epitomized. And herein, our spiritual flight to fullness expands to reach these greater heights when the anointing renders all yokes in our lives fruitless and void.

Finally, there's one more important note about this anointing upon the Christ and upon the Christians. It not only renders our lives free from yokes, it also renders the yokes in the people and environment around us powerless as well. This is why everywhere Jesus went the powers of darkness shook and shuttered.

This is shouting news for those of us who minister and live every day pressed by the contrary realities of sin, evil, sickness, poverty, oppression, depression, violence, and hopelessness. Like our Christ, the anointing within us can change the conditions around us.

In the Name of Jesus I declare the fullness of the power of the blessing of the Gospel in your life *and* the fullness of the power of the seven dimensions of the Holy Spirit to raise it up in you. You know the way.

Christ is the Way! Soar!

Scripture References